Dropshipping E-Commerce Business Model

The Ultimate Step-by-Step Guide for Beginners to Start Your E-commerce Business on Shopify, Amazon, or eBay and Make Money (Online from Home)

© **Copyright 2019 by Ronald Anderson- All rights reserved.**

The content contained within this book may not be reproduced, duplicated or transmitted without direct written permission from the author or the publisher.

Under no circumstances will any blame or legal responsibility be held against the publisher, or author, for any damages, reparation, or monetary loss due to the information contained within this book. Either directly or indirectly.

Legal Notice:

This book is copyright protected. This book is only for personal use. You cannot amend, distribute, sell, use, quote or paraphrase any part, or the content within this book, without the consent of the author or publisher.

Disclaimer Notice:

Please note the information contained within this document is for educational and entertainment purposes only. All effort has been executed to present accurate, up to date, and reliable, complete information. No warranties of any kind are declared or implied. Readers acknowledge that the author is not engaging in the rendering of legal, financial, medical or professional advice. The content within this book has been derived from various sources. Please consult a licensed professional before attempting any techniques outlined in this book.

By reading this document, the reader agrees that under no circumstances is the author responsible for any losses, direct or indirect, which are incurred as a result of the information contained within this document, including, but not limited to, — errors, omissions, or inaccuracies.

Table of Contents

Introduction 1

Chapter 1: Start from Scratch 2

Chapter 2: Reasons Why You Should Start a Dropshipping Business 9

Chapter 3: Benefits of the Dropshipping Business Model 13

Chapter 4: Drawbacks to Be Aware of 23

Chapter 5: Different Forms of Dropshipping 27

Chapter 6: Find Your Niche 41

Chapter 7: Source and Procure Top-Notch Suppliers 52

Chapter 8: Shopify 65

Chapter 9: eBay 80

Chapter 10: Amazon 96

Chapter 11: Your Own Dropshipping Website 115

Chapter 12: Your Online Presence 140

Chapter 13: Optimize Your Website for Selling 159

Chapter 14: How to Scale Your Dropshipping Business 173

Chapter 15: Pitfalls and Mistakes to Avoid 187

Conclusion 197

Introduction

To dropship or not to dropship, that is the question you need an answer to. This is what any entrepreneur asks him or herself when they decide to start a dropshipping business. Many people will immediately advise you to stay away from this business model as it is just a scam, or you will never make any money.

You are the captain of your own ship and you need to make an informed decision to start up your business. This is why this book sets out to take you as a beginner through the basics step-by-step to enable you to calmly and logically create your business. Your aim is success which you will achieve with the guidance given and starting on the right foot despite all the doomsday predictions of the nay-sayers who give unwanted bad advice.

So let's start with everything you need to know and understand and how to go about setting up your dropshipping business with the minimum fuss and bother.

Chapter 1: Start from Scratch

Starting out on the right foot and having all the important questions answers is essential to your success. Getting it right from the word go is far easier than trying to backtrack and fix the mistakes afterwards because you were to impatient or tried to take short cuts.

What Is Dropshipping?

Dropshipping is an e-commerce business model that differs from the conventional way of doing e-commerce in that you do not physically handle the products you sell, nor do you stockpile the products that you offer for sale. You set up your e-commerce shop online through your own website or using platforms such as Shopify, Amazon or eBay.

You offer certain products to your clients that are available from reliable wholesale suppliers and manufacturers that offer the products in your chosen niche. Once your client places the order with you, the chain reaction starts.

You in turn place an order with your supplier. Your supplier charges you for the product at a previously arranged price and then ships the product directly to your client.

Depending on your niche products, your suppliers can be anywhere on earth. There is no limitations of where your suppliers are located; this works for sensitive products as well as the timeframe from manufacture to delivery to client is shortened as inventory is not sitting on a shelf in the hopes of it being sold before expiry date.

When you decide on starting a business using the dropshipping business model, it changes how you do business and brings enormous flexibility to the daily operation of your company.

The Right Mindset Is Essential

To make a success of your dropshipping business you need to cultivate a strong entrepreneurial mindset right from the start. You cannot go into creating your own company with an apathetic and couldn't care less attitude. If you do, you are setting yourself up for failure. You must be hungry for success, you must go into this venture with a go-getter attitude and determination.

Commitment

You need to fully commit to this business venture and use all the resources available to you. The great thing is that you can fully commit to starting your dropshipping company even if you have another job; you do not have to give up one for the other. With commitment, you can juggle how you handle client enquiries and orders around your other job. Doing this allows you to start up your company and allow it to grow until you are comfortable to make the decision for a full changeover to running your company. If you fully commit from the beginning you will reap the benefits of having a smoothly running business that takes less time to maintain once it gains momentum.

Perseverance

We all live in an instant world where we expect gratification immediately for everything from food and entertainment to finances and anything we want to buy. We have grown so used to getting anything with the touch of a button or the click of a mouse. This unfortunately has cultivated a pampered and petulant mindset in many people that does not build strong character, commitment, and perseverance.

Perseverance is key to your success. There are many quotes and sayings about perseverance, about not giving up and try again if you do not succeed the first time. There is a good reason for these sayings as it means you are not the first person to come up against difficulties or problems, and those sayings were coined by people who persevered and kept going and tried until they found exactly what worked for them. Perseverance leads to determination; this leads to greater commitment to succeed and this is what you need from the start in setting up your own dropshipping business. No matter if things do not fall into place immediately, you just keep going until one by one each aspect of your business falls neatly into place.

No Quick Fix Attitude

There are no quick fixes when you start your own company. Trying to bypass necessary steps to save time and effort simply dooms this venture to failure. Do not be tempted by get-rich-quick scams that promise you a million dollar income with no effort, that does not exist. Get rid of any quick fix attitude that you may have, it will simply lead you to spend money fruitlessly and bypassing necessary steps in the startup phase of your business will be costly to correct later on. Do things right from the start and build your dropshipping business on a strong foundation that will be able to weather setbacks and whatever problems crop up as time goes on.

Invest Time and Energy

The phrase blood, sweat, and tears may sound overly dramatic, but you have to invest your time and energy to make a success of your dropshipping company. People far too often just want to throw large amounts of money into a business venture; you have no need to do that at all. Dropshipping gives you the chance to own your own business with limited capital by investing yourself and using your energy to get your business from the ground.

There are huge benefits to this form of investment that will profit you in the long run as your business grows.

- Your skills and knowledge will grow with your business as you gain firsthand experience of how each facet of your business operates.
- The skills you learn about operating your business is something that money cannot buy. When you start expanding, you will understand how each section of the company works and this is essential for managing other people that you will employ.
- You will get to know your customers and how they think and what they want. Markets are ever changing and being a hands on part of the running of the company you will get to know market trends to keep your customers happy. This will allow you to make decisions about suppliers to use and marketing strategies for your website to encourage potential customers to make use of your services.
- When you are an intimate part of the daily running of your company, you learn what to spend money on that is essential to the success of the business. Your mindset changes and your priorities shift away from non-essentials that may look nice or gadgets you can easily do without.

Focus on Solutions, Not Problems

Often, we focus so hard on a problem that occurred that we get bogged down in the details of the problem that we see no further. Turn your mindset around and start with, "I have to find a solution to this problem," instead of thinking, "I have a problem, I don't know what to do."

Train your mind to shift away from problems to see things from a solution perspective. Instead of worrying, turn to all the available avenues you have to find solutions. The internet provides you with knowledge literally at your fingertips. If you have a supplier problem, start searching for other suppliers. See what is available on Amazon, eBay, and Shopify and find out how you can utilize these platforms to your advantage to solve the problem you are experiencing. There are numerous blogs that focus on dropshipping and people share information and advice on how they solved their problems. The answers are out there, you simply have to invest some time to search for the best options that suit your needs.

Treat Mistakes as a Learning Curve, Not Failure

Mistakes are not the end of the world; there is no human on the planet who can say that they have never made any mistakes in their lives. Mistakes happen in every type of business there is. How you handle the mistake and what you do about it makes a huge difference though.

A mistake does not mean you are a complete failure and should just close up your new dropshipping company. Each mistake gives you the opportunity to learn. You will learn to find solutions and different ways to avoid this particular mistake in future.

Mistakes teach you valuable lessons in customer care. You learn to admit mistakes and how to placate irate customers without losing that customer. Every customer care situation you have to handle improve your customer care skills and will benefit you in the future.

A mistake involving a supplier lets you hone your skills in cooperation and negotiation that benefits your business and the business of your supplier.

Chapter 2: Reasons Why You Should Start a Dropshipping Business

Is It Really Worth Your Time and Effort?

The answer is a resounding yes. As with starting any type of business, you will not get a stress-free way to generate income. You will have to work hard and be committed to your business venture. You can expect the outcome to clearly show the effort and time that you are willing to put into this.

The reality that all businesses face today is that we operate is a world that has changed vastly over the past few decades. Strategies that worked 30 years ago are now obsolete, and if you hope to be competitive and successful, you need to adjust and grow to keep up with how the advances in technology has influenced how people shop.

People no longer want to have to physically go to shops and be limited to what is available in that specific store. Everyone has time constraints and want to get as much accomplished in a day as possible, so it is far more convenient to grab a smartphone or laptop to get their shopping done.

E-commerce has taken over the world and the dropshipping business model fits in well as the world markets move faster.

The retail giants of a few decades ago are floundering as people now prefer to shop online and have their purchases delivered to them directly. This is understandable because e-commerce has introduced shoppers to global shopping.

This chart provided by Business Insider and correlated from data within their company shows the grim reality that traditional retailers face. The chart clearly shows why it is worth your time and effort to start your own dropshipping company.

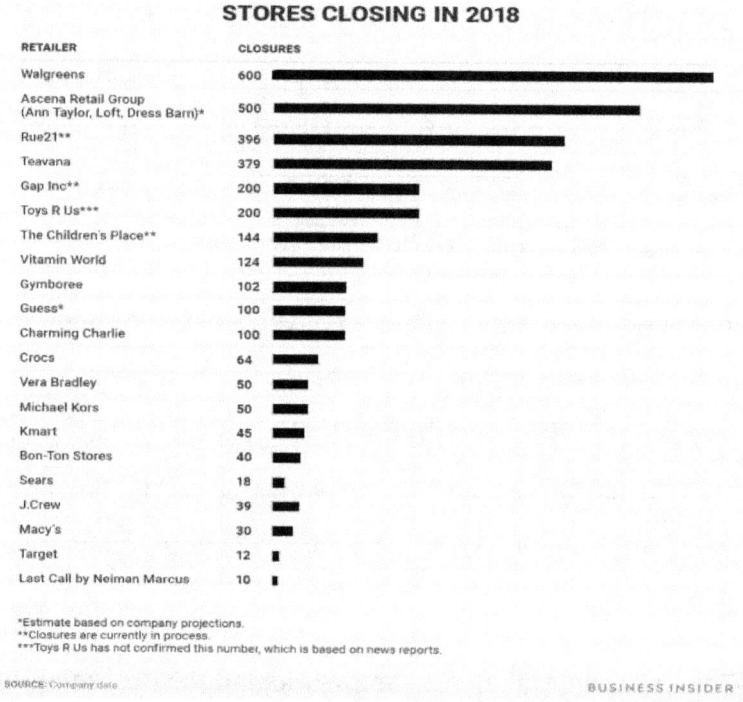

(Business Insider, 2018)

Chapter 3: Benefits of the Dropshipping Business Model

A dropshipping business is radically different from traditional retail outlets as you do not operate from a physical business premises and that completely changes how you operate. Dropshipping also differs from conventional e-commerce business in that these businesses buy inventory and send out purchases to clients from their inventory.

Dropshipping has an impressive number of benefits that are specific to the dropshipping business model.

Less Capital Investment

Yes, you need some capital to start a business. The big difference is that you do not need huge amounts of money to start your dropshipping business. You only need some cash as a safety net during the time you work towards getting your company operational. All businesses have minor running costs, and you need to be aware that you should set some money aside for web hosting costs and any fees payable for making use of dropshipping platforms. It is wise to have cash on hand for incidental expenses. Keeping this in mind will minimize stress and you can focus on getting your business off the ground.

Easy to Start Up

You do not physically carry stock so you do not need a warehouse to house inventory. This means you have no costs associated with a warehouse, such as property rental and warehouse equipment. This also eliminates all the complications inherent in managing a warehouse. No valuable hours are lost in re-ordering stock and having to keep strict accounting of inventory movement.

You are not responsible for packing, labeling, and shipping of the products you sell, nor do you handle inbound product shipments or returns. This makes it far easier to start up your business and removes the logistical nightmare of packaging and shipping from your life.

Overheads

Overheads are a nightmare that companies deal with on a daily basis. The dropshipping business model eliminates the majority of overhead expenses as you can start and run your business from home. As your company grows, it is normal that your overhead expenses increase, but your costs will always be far below the overhead costs for a traditional retail outlet.

Location

Having a dropshipping business gives you most flexibility regarding your location and you can run your business literally from any place where you have access to the internet. You have no need for fancy and expensive offices to impress potential customers; you just need a laptop and internet, which is ideal as you conduct business with equal ease whether you sit at a desk at home or traveling.

Global Market

E-commerce and using the dropshipping business format gives you access to markets around the world; you are not limited to local products in your country. Dropshipping is done with equal ease from any supplier and manufacturer worldwide. This is very appealing to customers as they have a much wider range to choose from than would ever be possible from any retailer in their area.

This graph shows the immense popularity of e-commerce around the world. With the online retail platforms, you gain easy access to global markets for your dropshipping business.

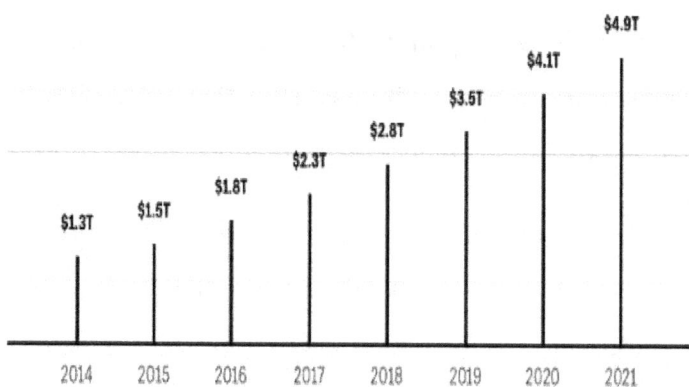

(MGR Consulting Group, n.d.)

Extensive Product Availability in Your Niche

Niche products can often be very restrictive as to choice of what products you can add to your e-commerce business as only certain suppliers may carry the products that you need. If you were only restricted to local markets, this would cause huge problems, limit the growth of your business, and negatively impact on your profit margin. Access to global markets is a total game changer for niche products, making this a top benefit for all sellers that specialize in niche products.

Substantial Lower Risk Factors

Dropshipping instead of the more conventional e-commerce business model is a huge benefit in lowering the risks of monetary loss to the dropshipping seller as you do not run the risk of not being able to sell the inventory you have already paid for. Should you hit a slow time and not make a sale, the only monetary loss is the potential profit you could have made on a sale.

Another factor that lowers the risk is that you only place the order with your supplier once your customer has placed an order with you and paid for it. You use the money already paid to you when you contact your supplier and not your own money, so you do not have to always make sure you have extra funds when you place an order with your supplier.

Win-win Situation for Supplier and Dropshipping Business

Suppliers and manufacturers are keen to work with dropshipping companies because the more people they can get to sell their products, the bigger their overall profits will be. Suppliers are willing to negotiate a better or a wholesale price with dropshipping companies even though the dropshipping businesses do not buy his products in bulk.

The reasons for their keenness is that they get wider exposure for their products with no marketing costs to themselves, plus it gives them more time to produce their goods. Suppliers are very aware that building up a good relationship with the dropshipping business means that the company will keep coming back to them to purchase more products at a good price.

This is a win-win situation for everyone with a more productive supplier and a loyal dropshipping company that keeps a steady flow of orders coming in, resulting in raised profit for supplier and dropshipping business.

Using Online Retail Platforms

Making use of the online retail platforms is an important part of the success of your dropshipping business. We will discuss the online retail platforms in detail in later chapters and look at the general benefits here.

Exposure to Unlimited Customers

The aim of every online store is to get exposure to as many potential customers as possible. When you join up with the online retail platforms, you immediately get exposure to virtually unlimited customers without having to spend huge amounts of money on marketing.

A Vast Range of Products to Choose from in Your Niche

Another huge benefit of using the online retail platforms is the huge range of products on offer that fall within your niche, you can pick and choose what you feel suits you best and if you find a specific chosen product is not selling very well, it is easy to switch to another product on offer on the platform. Experimenting with which products sell the best is not a costly venture when you use the retail platforms as you have no losses with inventory that is not selling. Keeping track of your selling trends enables you to switch and change fast to keep on top of your game.

Multitude of Vacant Niches

The giant retail platforms such as Amazon, Shopify, and eBay always have a large number of vacant niches for you to explore, which is a golden opportunity for you to expand your business into more than one niche. The retail platforms do the leg work and your company reaps the benefits without you spending manhours and manpower researching new opportunities.

Scaling

What is scaling with regards to a dropshipping company and how does it work? This is one of the questions most frequently asked by entrepreneurs starting their own dropshipping company.

Scaling up your dropshipping business means growing and expanding. Scaling this business model is far easier than for traditional e-commerce business because for the traditional business model it means a lot more work, the more orders received, the more work is involved.

For a dropshipping business, the process works differently. Your dropshipping suppliers do most of the work generated to process more orders, making the growing process for you easier and eliminating most of the growing pains other companies have to deal with.

Chapter 4: Drawbacks to Be Aware of

All business models have pros and cons, it is the same with the dropshipping model. This does not mean it is a bad business model, simply that you should be aware of drawbacks that are specific to dropshipping. You make allowances for the drawbacks, try to avoid those you can and find solutions around problems wherever possible. Facing drawbacks does not mean your business is a failure, you can overcome many drawbacks by planning ahead and putting backup solutions in place.

Margins Are Low

Many people are put off by the low margins in their chosen niche. People want to see higher profits and grow their business faster. If you are prepared to start small, persevere, and get to know everything about operating a dropshipping business in the very competitive field of e-commerce, you will grow steadily and reap the benefits of your hard work.

Competition in the Market Place

E-commerce is very competitive and sellers undercut each other to make money faster. Dropshipping companies are easy to set up with a small cash startup, making it a very competitive business model. The best way to deal with this is by starting up your business correctly, give quality service to your customers, and use all the resources available to you to develop a good business reputation.

Issues with Inventory and Product Fulfillment

As a dropshipping business model, you do not control your own inventory and you are not able to keep track of the flow of stock. You depend on suppliers and wholesalers that service many other merchants as well. This can create issues with products being out of stock when you place your order.

Your suppliers are in charge of product fulfillment and mistakes and delays in shipping can occur. You will have to deal with your irate customers, so it is wise to develop as many backup supplies as you can to accommodate your customers with alternative products.

Online Retail Platforms

Online retail platforms are a great benefit for dropshipping companies, but it can also be a drawback as customers can go around you and purchase the same products directly on the retail platforms.

Shipping Can Become Complex

Dropshipping companies normally source their products through several different suppliers and wholesalers. Shipping to customers can become complex with multiple item orders that are sourced from more than one supplier. You then will have a separate shipping charge for each item of the multiple product order, and you cannot pass the extra costs on to your customer, you will have to bear the extra costs. This cuts into your profit margin.

Suppliers Can Make Mistakes

Suppliers make mistakes and when that happens you will be blamed. The responsibility is yours as the customer put the order in with you, not with your supplier. Supplier mistakes can be for various reasons, some legitimate mistakes, others caused by problems within the supplier's own company.

To minimize mistakes of shoddy workmanship, below standard packing materials, and shipments being damaged or lost, you have to source your suppliers carefully. Should suppliers let you down through negligence, you should switch to a reputable supplier immediately as these mistakes reflect badly on you. Your business reputation is incredibly important and you do not want to damage this.

Scaling Abilities of Suppliers

Not all suppliers are equally competent and some may not have the ability to keep up with scaling as your company grows. The great news is that you have access to suppliers around the world as well as the online retail platforms to source your products, so it is very easy to switch suppliers.

Chapter 5: Different Forms of Dropshipping

The dropshipping business model started out very basic. It was more of a service than a full business model where product manufacturers and wholesale companies offered a dropshipping service to suppliers. The suppliers would then ship products to customers one by one as and when customers placed an order for a specific product.

The dropshipping business model evolved from that to where dropshipping has become a standalone complete business. We now have several forms of the dropshipping business model with variations as per the needs of individual businesses.

From Suppliers

This is the most personal form of the dropshipping business model where interaction with the suppliers is by phone and email. Terms and contracts, interactions with the support team, all the negotiations are done with real people, not with automated systems.

Benefits

Sustainable business

Building business relationships with suppliers creates a maintainable business that is long term. With this form of dropshipping, your supplier is much more approachable and accommodating when problems pop up or when new products come online. Many dropshipping companies prefer this type of dropshipping as they are more comfortable with personal relationships than the anonymity of using the e-commerce online retail platforms.

Mutual Interests

It is normal for any business to experience problems and having a personal relationship with a supplier changes how problems are resolved. It is to the mutual benefit of the supplier and the dropshipping company to work together to resolve problems in a positive way. It is not simply a case of you losing a sale and making no profit. The supplier is aware of the impact each lost sale has on his own business.

Drawbacks

Difficult to Find

When you use online retail platforms everything is impersonal, you approach any of the large number of online platforms that is easily available on the internet. When you use suppliers you have to put in a lot of work to find a supplier you can fully trust, who is professional and reliable. Should anything happen to your supplier, you are left in limbo until you can source another reliable supplier.

Human Error

Human error can spell disaster for a dropshipping company. Suppliers who are not vigilant and maintain tight control over their inventory could have far reaching consequences for you and the reputation of your business.

When an e-commerce order is placed it constitutes a binding legal contract between you as the seller and your customer. It is deemed completely unprofessional for a seller to cancel an order and will result in a negative by the customer on your website and on social media. When this happens, the dropshipping seller tries to avoid this and, as an emergency measure, place an order for the specific item on one of the online retail platforms or an alternative supplier, most often at a higher price. You have to inform your customer of the delay in shipping their order, which could cause the loss of a return customer.

Relationships Are Hard Work

When you choose to use suppliers for your dropship business you will have to maintain constant communication. You cannot build a solid working relationship with your suppliers if you keep to minimal contact through phone and email and whatever chat apps they use. This is time-consuming and some people find this off-putting and prefer the fast, automated communication that you have with the online retail platforms.

Setting Up a Store On an Online Retail Platform

Using an online retail platform is the easiest and fastest way to get your dropshipping business off the ground and operating. It is important to know that the online retail platforms do not operate the same. Each platform has different rules and policies. You need to do research into each of these platforms to find the one that fit all your specific needs, are the most cost effective for your dropshipping business with the most benefits.

Timeframe to Set Up

The major retail platforms offer to get your store set up and operational within 24 hours, making this a huge plus point. First-time entrepreneurs are still trying to find their feet in their venture into business and most often do not have the knowledge and resources to start up on their own. So, being able to see their store and start organizing and selling in such a short time is valuable to them.

Immediate Audience

Immediate access to a huge audience in their niche instead of laboriously setting up their own website and struggling to gain decent search engine ranking. E-commerce can be overwhelming to inexperienced dropshipping business owners as most start with an idea they want to grow into a sustainable business. Your chosen niche may be absolutely great, but all the intricacies of the process can be daunting. Getting access to all that the retail platforms offer makes taking the first steps into dropshipping manageable.

Marketing

Marketing can turn into a nightmare for most people unless you are an experienced professional marketer. Outsourcing the marketing for your business is costly and absorbs whatever cash you have set aside, money you could spend much better on other aspects of your business. Signing up with an online retail platform of your choice takes the huge burden of marketing off your shoulders.

Apps and Automation Possibilities

Dropshipping from online platforms give you access to a large number of apps that you would not have access to for free or for a low cost if you have to invest in these apps for your own dropshipping website. E-commerce relies heavily on apps, and in today's competitive markets, many apps are essential to running a business smoothly.

Drawbacks

Many drawbacks to selling through the retail platforms are specific to how each of them operate. There are some general drawbacks though, across the board, that affect your cash flow, is time consuming, and can impact your business negatively.

Multiple Fees

There are multiple fees involved when you dropship through the retail portals and these add up to a significant amount. Some of the platforms have more charges according to how the specific retail platform operates. These are some of the fees you should be aware of:

- Subscription fees that vary according to the plan you choose and the perks of specific plans.
- Listing fees.

- Final value fee (eBay).

No Real Individuality

The online retail portal is in control of what your store looks like, what marketing is applied, as well as branding. There is no scope for individuality and customization.

No Connection with Customers

As there is no personal interactions with customers, you do not build rapport with them. You are just a disembodied e-commerce store on a computer screen to them. You do not build up any long-term connection with customers and they feel that they owe you no loyalty or consideration.

Not Building an Asset

Your business is an asset in which you invest time, energy and money to build up. When you dropship through suppliers and your own website, the business is an asset with a sales value should you decide to sell it at a later stage. Your online store on the retail platforms stop existing when you close your account.

Arbitrage Dropshipping

This form of dropshipping has been in the news a lot lately and is being debated heavily. The online retail platforms do not approve of arbitrage selling. To choose this form of dropshipping, you need to understand how it differs from other forms and all the pros and cons that come specifically with arbitrage selling.

Arbitrage dropshipping is basically playing one retail platform against another retail platform. Arbitrage sellers do not source suppliers and list those products on the retail platform in their stores.

For example, Platform A lists a product for $10 and Platform B lists the same item for a higher price. The arbitrage seller buys the product at the lower price on Platform A and provides the delivery address of the buyer on Platform B. Platform A then delivers the product to what is in fact Platform B's customer. The arbitrage dropshipper pockets the difference between the lower and higher prices listed.

Benefits

Numerous Suppliers

For the majority of products available through e-commerce there will be numerous suppliers on the retail platform listing the same products, though prices can vary from supplier to supplier. This means you can easily switch between suppliers, depending who has the specific product available that you want at any specific time. You keep your customers happy as they do not have to wait for stock availability and a delay in delivery.

No Delay in Entering the Market

Everything you need is already in place. You need no time to set up a website and cultivate relationships with suppliers. You simply have to compare the prices for specific items between the retail platforms and you can start taking orders.

Automation

With the very large variety of tools available for automation, most of the aspects of your business can run automatically once you have set up shop, leaving you with more than enough time to give great customer care.

Drawbacks

Sustainability

This form of dropshipping is not a sustainable model in the long run. The absolute ease with which anyone can set up this dropshipping business model attracts large numbers of people who want to make as much money as possible in the shortest timespan. This fierce competition results in ever shrinking profit margins. This means you have to aim to sell more and more to break even. With such a small profit margin there is no room for cancelled orders or delivery problems as you simply do not have the cash flow to cope with these problems.

Not Possible Without Automation

The competition in this form of dropshipping is so fierce that it is no longer to do this without every possible form of automation available. You are not only competing with other companies in your specific niche, but also with bulk sellers that list literally thousands of products that will also include your niche products. Basically everybody is climbing on the bandwagon and there is only X amount of profit to be made, so individual profits keep shrinking.

Not in the Best Interest of Retail Platforms

Arbitrage dropshipping has become very controversial for the online retail platforms as it has a negative impact on their client base. The platforms do not have a problem with the dropshipping business model, but with arbitrage dropshipping playing one platform against another. There are such a flood of people doing arbitrage selling that is is noticeable to customers. Customers start investigating when their purchase from Platform B is delivered with the packaging of Platform A. They then change which platform they do their online purchasing from in the future.

Using Amazon Fulfillment Service

Dropshipping on Amazon is legal, but Amazon does not encourage the traditional form of dropshipping. Dropshipping businesses have always operated by sourcing products from suppliers that offer their niche products. The tasks of physically handling the products rest upon the shoulders of the supplier and the supplier handles the storage, packaging, and shipping.

With the FBA system, the dropshipping business must purchase minimum order sizes from the original supplier, and it goes into storage in one of the Amazon warehouses. Amazon becomes your dropshipper instead of the original supplier that you purchased the products from.

The FBA system has numerous advantages for the dropshipping company by taking over the functions the supplier normally would perform. You as the reseller have access to all the features and tools available to all owners of Amazon stores plus being part of the most recognizable brand globally.

This dropshipping model is daunting for many entrepreneurs. Instead of the traditional dropshipping model with very low startup costs, they must invest in inventory and face many costs they may not be financially prepared for when they are just starting out.

Please see Chapter 10 for the full details, fees, and policies regarding the use of the Fulfilled by Amazon dropshipping business model.

Chapter 6: Find Your Niche

For a dropshipping company to be successful, you cannot afford to offer general products over a wide spectrum. There is simply too much competition from retailers, other e-commerce businesses, and the online retail platforms.

What Is a Niche?

You need to specialize and focus on a specific product or a specific niche and focus only on products that fall within your chosen niche. It is simply not economically viable for a dropshipping business to grab around for products that catch the eye, or a trend that is popular at the moment.

To determine which niche amongst the nearly countless niches available globally can be tricky and deciding on one specific niche to specialize in can feel overpowering for anyone new to the dropshipping business model. We will take you through the best guidelines that will help you enormously to find the niche that is right for you.

What Are You Passionate About and Interests You?

Jot down a list of things you feel passionate about, things that interest you greatly that could be a niche for your dropshipping business. It is important to choose a niche that you can relate to. You need to understand the product and sell to customers with confidence knowing that you will be able to advise customers in a professional manner if they have questions.

If you feel strongly about the niche you choose you will have greater perseverance and determination to succeed even when problems crop up. If you really don't care at all about the products you sell, it will be far easier to quit at the first bump in the road.

Many dropshipping companies have been started through the hobby of the owner that turned into a successful business where products are on offer to people who have similar interests.

Research Is Key to Your Success

It is one thing to be passionate and knowledgeable about the niche you want, but you are starting a business that must be profitable. To determine if your niche will create an income stream for you, you must backup your choice with in-depth research.

Scrutinize the Top Products in Your Niche

Go to websites like ClickBank, Simple Goods, Selify for example and do a search for the products you want to sell in your dropshipping business. The more you find your niche products on offer, the better as it shows a demand. Should you find these websites have none of your niche goods on offer, it shows that your niche products are not in demand and has not been monetized successfully by someone else.

Google Tools

Use Google Keyword Planner and Google Trends to search keywords and keyword combinations relating to your niche. Google tools will provide you with information about how often your keywords are being searched through search engines. Google tools have various search options available for you to explore and determine the demand for your niche products through searches made by people.

Google Trends analyze trends in online searches being made and tracks changes in the volume of searches over periods of time. Statistics gathered by Google Trends show any seasonal trends for the product search terms you used. This gives you good insight into whether your nice products will have periods of high demand and at other times during the year slow down, which indicates that income from your niche products will fluctuate. Google Trends also provide data on the locations from where searches are made for the keywords pertaining to your niche products.

Social Media

Social media is very powerful and can be very helpful when you must decide which niche will work best for you. Look on Facebook and check what is being said about your niche, how people are talking about your niche, and look for groups and forums.

Shipping Costs

Shipping costs play a big role in your profit margin. If it is too high, your markup will push your selling prices up too much and prospective customers will look for cheaper options elsewhere. Low shipping costs can also be used as a marketing strategy and promotional tool if you can absorb the shipping costs instead of passing it along with a substantial mark up in price. Free shipping catches the attention of customers immediately and will lead to an increase in sales.

Profit Margin

It is very important to keep in mind that the amount of work you put in to sell an inexpensive product is exactly the same as the effort put in to market high-priced items. It is therefore worthwhile to look for a niche with high-end products as this will improve your profit margin overall.

Size and Weight

Too often when deciding to start a dropshipping company, people forget about the physical size of the products they want to sell, and the weight of the product. Shipping costs are annoying and everyone tries to avoid it at all costs. This is very important as you can easily see your profits disappearing like mist if your chosen niche products incur huge shipping costs.

Legal Marketing

Research the products you want to sell in depth and make very sure that you will not have any legal issues. You must be able to sell your chosen niche products anywhere. It is crucial that you are able to sell on online retail platforms, your own website, and through social media without worries about whether you will get shut down for infringing any state or country laws.

Impulse Buyers

A huge percentage of online shoppers see something they like and they impulsively buy the item. Online shopping has changed how people shop as they literally have the world of shopping at their fingertips. When choosing your niche, you should take this into account and the products you sell should be appealing to the impulse buyers.

By selling products that appeal to impulse buyers, you immediately broaden your customer base significantly. Yes, it is true, impulse buyers most often do not become return customers. When you calculate over a period of time how much income you generate through this type of sales, you will be surprised at how much it adds up to.

Strategize

Personal Interest

When you are really interested in something, your general knowledge of the subject will be far more extensive in comparison to choosing a niche and products that you have no interest in and have no knowledge about. Starting your product search from a strong foundation of interest and knowledge make the search more productive. You will be able to discard products faster that you are not passionate about, or products of low quality that will not sell very well.

Professional Experience

Another strategy in the search for the best products to sell is to look at things from having professional experience with such products. You may not be passionate about the products, but instead have good knowledge about how it works and what the pros and cons of the products are. You may have encountered the products through your own experiences with them, or through your job. The main thing here is that you will be able to answer questions from customers with confidence and give answers that are knowledgeable and factual. Another advantage of choosing products from a professional viewpoint is that you will know where there are gaps in the marketplace and where there is a definite need for products in that industry.

Trends Versus Fads

Fads come and go, what could be the most popular today and be pushed aside tomorrow. Your goal is to make money, so to capitalize you must first be able to separate fad from trend. Fads are gimmicks that are non essentials and easily forgotten.

When you look at trendy products to add to your niche, ask yourself two questions. Does this product fulfill a need for people, and does the product solve a problem for users. A trend fills a need or solves a problem whereas a fad is interesting or fun for a few weeks or months and then people grow bored and move onto something else that catch their attention.

What Frustrates and Annoys People?

Research your products by putting yourself in the shoes of a customer. What annoyances and frustrations do people have that they have to contend with day in and day out. The criteria is to find products that will make things easier for customers, and something they would definitely want to buy.

Hobbies and Interest of Others

You do not have to be personally interested in a subject, instead do research into the hobbies and interests of other people that has a market for the products related to their interests. The best place to start is by doing a search for hobbies, top hobbies, or trendy hobbies.

Another place you will find great information is going through hobby magazines, especially hobbies that have dedicated magazines. Another research tool is going through social media groups. See what they are talking about, what they are buying and the jargon used. Note down words specific to a hobby, those are invaluable search words to use.

Learn about the people who have specific hobbies as everything you learn about your potential customer base can be used as marketing strategies for products they are especially interested in.

Local Availability

For your dropshipping company to be economically viable, you need to choose your niche wisely. If your niche products are available freely at local retailers, people will simply pop out and pick up the items from their nearest shop. Humans are impatient and will not wait for products to be shipped to them if they can easily pick it up on their way home from work.

You have access to global markets which broadens your supplier base greatly and with research you will be able to find a great niche and products that customers want that they cannot get at local stores.

Check What Your Competition Is Up To

It is easy to fall into the trap of thinking that if there is very little or no competition for the niche you want, then that is great and you will dominate the market in your niche. Do some research and see what competition you are up against because there are usually good reasons why other companies are not offering these specific products.

The reasons vary from the fact that there simply is no demand for these products or there is so little profit to be made that other companies moved away from these items. It may also be that the shipping and packing costs are prohibitive or that production issues are so problematic that it is not profitable to invest in these products.

Your need to take all of the above factors into consideration when deciding on the best niche for you. You may not like having to compete, but competition means that the products are highly in demand and with these products your company is sustainable in the long run.

Chapter 7: Source and Procure Top-Notch Suppliers

Not all suppliers are the same, some are excellent, or good while others are mediocre or worse. This is the reality that face all new dropshipping companies and you need to know right from the start what to look for in suppliers, how to handle suppliers and what you need to avoid.

Be Legal Before You Contact Suppliers

You need to set your business up correctly in all legal aspects and have all your paperwork in place when you start sourcing and contacting potential suppliers and wholesalers. This is essential as suppliers will ask for proof of your legality before they will consider doing business with you. It is okay to start asking basic questions, suppliers are used to entrepreneurs looking for information and will give you answers without demanding proof that you are a legal company.

Suppliers and wholesalers will not do business with companies they have not approved, and for that approval to be granted, you need to be legally incorporated and have complied with all state laws. Sadly, the wholesalers have learned the hard way that too many people try to scam them. So, make sure all your paperwork is in order and you will start out by building up good relationships with your suppliers.

Successful Online Search for Suppliers

Suppliers and wholesalers are known to be quirky and very individualistic and to find the ones you really want to do business with will take some innovative searching. It is not the case that suppliers are trying to hide away from entrepreneurs, they simply march to their own drummers. You therefore need to do some serious searches and use the following guidelines to achieve the best results.

In-Depth Searches

Suppliers do not consider marketing to be a top priority for their products. You will have to patiently dig through a large number of search results to find the information you need. Most often the official website of the supplier will only be found for example on Page 6 or Page 10 of the search results when searching for a specific product. Persevere and you will reap the benefits.

Modify Your Search Criteria

You must modify your searches, it is not enough to just search for supplier X or product Y. Your search results will be mediocre at best. Make lists of synonyms for example for wholesaler and supplier and do a search on each of the synonyms. Use alternative wording and different search phrases to get the best search results.

Functional, Not Appealing

Usually when you land on a website you look for things that you find appealing, items that catch your eye immediately and websites hold your attention with snappy web content and high quality photos.

Wholesalers and suppliers have websites that are minimalistic and functional and often look quite old fashioned and antiquated, especially to young entrepreneurs . They are fully aware that clients need them and will look for them so they do not waste their valuable time and resources in creating websites to entice potential clients. Learn to look past the outward appearance of their websites, it is not an indication of a bad supplier or mediocre products on offer.

Convenience of Paid Supplier Directories

Making use of supplier directories is a topic heavily debated as some people feel that it is an extravagance and something you won't be using again once you have settled upon your suppliers. There is no right or wrong answer, it is a personal choice each entrepreneur makes.

These databases are extremely convenient to have on hand as they are organized and categorized so you have all the suppliers together for specific products and regularly updated. Most of the top organizations that offer paid supplier directories also screen the companies before they enter them into the directories to ensure that all their listings are legitimately operating suppliers and wholesalers.

Another benefit of using paid directories is that you have access to a large number of alternative suppliers for your niche products should you have an emergency and need to switch suppliers quickly.

Supplier directories are not an essential necessity for your business but a reliable and convenient tool to have when you need it or when you want to start scaling your business.

A Trick of the Trade to Keep Handy

When you are really in a bind, you can use the well known trick of placing a very small order with one of your competitors in the dropshipping businesses. This can really help you if you if you need to find a supplier but have been unsuccessful.

Once you have received your order from your competitor, it is quick and easy to do an internet search of the return address on your package and it will give you the info of who originally shipped the package to you.

Build Credibility with Suppliers

Credibility is a vital currency in the ever-changing world of e-commerce that you must have to make a success of your dropshipping business. To understand how important this is, you have to put yourself in the shoes of suppliers and wholesalers. They constantly have to deal with eager entrepreneurs who may or may never become their client. They do not have the time or inclination to deal with persons who are not even sure of what they want and often try to use the supplier as a free sounding board to answer questions and give free advice.

Be decisive and professional when approaching a supplier. Do not be vague about your business goals and do not start demanding terms and discounts when you have not even started placing orders with them.

Credibility cannot be demanded, it has to be earned through interaction with the supplier over a period of time. Should you be overbearing and demanding when you are just starting out with a supplier you will be labeled as an annoying upstart to be avoided whenever possible and you will not be able to shake off that negative reputation easily.

Get Personal, Pick Up the Phone

We live in a world of instant communication via email, chat programs and social media without ever having personal contact with people. When you are sourcing a new supplier, change your mindset and make personal contact by picking up the phone. Speak to them, hear their voice, and you will find people are far more approachable than keeping it impersonal words on a screen.

Suppliers are used to answering questions from customers and will accommodate you, and this will help to build a good rapport between you and the supplier. If this is a new supplier and you feel nervous approaching him for the first time, makes notes of questions you need answers to.

Place Test Orders

When you want to place orders with a new supplier, it is good business sense to not jump in blindly, for even if you had done in-depth research and feel confident in the ability of the supplier to complete order fulfillment successfully, you need to test the waters.

Place small orders for the first few orders so that you can observe how this specific supplier or wholesaler operates his business. This will enable you to observe how smooth the ordering process is handled by the company and the time taken to ship orders to your customers. Take note of how quickly the supplier issues tracking data and how efficient the company billing department is in issuing an invoice to you.

You can get feedback from your customers regarding the packaging used and gauge their satisfaction with packaging, shipping and delivery.

Attributes to Look for in Suppliers

When you select your suppliers you need to be sure that they are reputable and reliable. You cannot entrust the success of your business to a supplier who is careless or has a reputation for being late with shipments. Suppliers play a vital part in any dropshipping business and you must know the supplier is dependable. So, when you must decide if a specific supplier will perform his role successfully, use the criteria below as your yardstick. What you should aim for is that your intended supplier has most of the needed attributes, if not all.

Well Trained and Informed Members of Staff

Competent suppliers that have experienced staff who are able to professionally answer questions about the products they sell. If the sales staff cannot fully answer questions about the industry they represent or the different products they market, it reflects badly on whether the supplier operates a well-run company. You need a supplier you can rely on, especially when you are a new business or when you start scaling into a new niche you do not have detailed knowledge of.

Up-To-Date Technology

All the forms of e-commerce rely heavily on modern technology. Make sure that the prospective supplier has kept up with the technology needed to make the process from ordering through shipping to delivery run smoothly.

The supplier's website does not need to be fancy; instead, it has to be super functional, so check whether he has invested in the following necessities for online trading.

- All-inclusive online catalog.

- Data feeds that can be customized to suit the specific needs of clients.
- Accessible real-time inventory.

Location, If Using Suppliers Inside the Country

When you make use of supplies that are local, you need to look at exactly where the supplier is located. The more central the supplier's location it, the more beneficial it is for your business. It is well-known that local shipping very often takes longer than shipping into the country from overseas. If your supplier is central, it cuts down significantly on shipping time. Less shipping time often means lower shipping fees and happier clients.

Preferred Method of Placing Orders

Find out the various ways that the supplier accepts orders. You do not want to be restricted to placing all your orders telephonically. This is not very convenient as you are restricted to business hours only.

Should you be limited to only placing orders manually through the supplier's website, the ordering process is slow and takes a lot of time. You need the third option of placing orders via email to free up more time that you can spend productively doing other tasks.

Dedicated Support Staff to Deal with You

If you have to deal with a different support staff member each time you have to call the supplier, it becomes very frustrating. You have to repeat yourself over and over as the staff you deal with has no knowledge of the reason you called before. This is hugely problematic when you need to resolve any problems and time-consuming. A competent supplier will allocate a specific support member of staff who deals with your orders and queries.

Suppliers and Wholesalers to Avoid

There are several revealing indicators to warn you to steer clear of a specific supplier or wholesaler. Rather look for another supplier who operates his business ethically and without does not pressure clients with dishonest schemes. Be vigilant and avoid getting involved with suppliers as soon as you pick up any of these signs.

Negative Reviews

Check the supplier's website for negative feedback given by previous clients and check social media to see how many complaints clients have had. Consumer complaints websites give you a good idea of the reviews and feedback concerning a supplier.

Bulk Quantity Products

Companies that specialize in the sale of very cheap bulk products does not inspire confidence as a preferred supplier for your dropshipping business.

Demanding Ongoing Fees to Be Able to Do Business with Them

Suppliers who demand ongoing fees from you for the "privilege" of doing business with them are to be avoided at all costs. This is a form of coercion that you should not fall prey to.

Abnormally High Pre-Order Fees

Pre-order fees are a part of life for all dropshipping businesses and these fees fluctuate according to the type of order you place regarding the size of the order, whether it is a bulk order or a very complex order. What is not normal is a supplier that charges pre-order fees that are far higher than the norm; this is not an ethical business practice.

Non-Negotiable Minimum Size Policy

If a supplier is not willing to be flexible regarding his minimum size order policy, this company is not suitable for your dropshipping business. Many suppliers are prepared to charge you the minimum size fee upfront and then fulfill your order quantities over time as your customers place orders with you. Make sure about what you can expect before you start using a supplier.

Chapter 8: Shopify

Dropshipping businesses rely on the online e-commerce retail platforms as an integral part of their business. The e-commerce online platforms do not have a standardized way of operating, each have their own operating methods and pros and cons. Shopify is one of the most popular platforms to use for several reasons.

What is Shopify?

Shopify is a comprehensive online retail platform. For a monthly subscription fee, you create an online store on the platform from where you can market and sell your products globally. Shopify has brought together an impressive set of tools to assist you in setting up your store with integration of numerous payment gateways and supports in excess of 50 languages.

Shopify offers around the clock support to all customers with 24/7 phone support as well as live chat to assist with any problems that may arise.

Benefits of Using Shopify in Your Dropshipping Business

For Beginners

The e-commerce platforms can be overwhelming for anyone starting out in the dropshipping business and Shopify makes it as easy as possible. They offer tools to help you set up your Shopify account and are very dropshipping friendly.

To assist new clients, Shopify regularly post tutorials to assist customers in using the retail platform as well as case studies to assist people with questions. They also post success stories regularly to encourage new entrepreneurs who may have doubts about starting out in business.

Free and Paid-For Templates and Themes

Shopify has a huge variety of professional themes and templates available that are ready to use when you set up your Shopify store. The templates are customer orientated and mobile-ready. All the templates are extremely responsive and easy to operate. A huge plus for a person starting out in dropshipping is that you are not restricted to only paid for templates and themes. The free templates work great and you do not have to fork out extra cash right from the start. You have to option to upgrade to paid for themes and templates at a later stage if you want to have more extra features and enhanced customization.

SEO Functions Are Built-In

All forms of e-commerce is very competitive and fast growing. You need all the help and support you can get to make it easier to succeed. The majority of entrepreneurs are not SEO experts and this can be a very time-consuming part of their business. Shopify takes all the hard work out of SEO for you by giving you all the features you need to make you very visible to search engines and be indexed. Search engine visibility is a critical necessity for any business today.

Features available to use are:

- Adding and editing of meta tags.
- Ability to add product descriptions.
- Arranging products in collections.

Cross Channel Sales

The ability to do cross channel selling is a huge boost for your business. You can connect your Shopify store with a Facebook page and use the Shopify app for direct sales, thereby increasing your potential client base hugely. Social networking is incredibly powerful as a marketing tool and you can do cross channel sales on other platforms, such as Twitter and Pinterest. Do some research and find those platforms that allow cross channel sales.

An Extensive App Store

To assist their clients, Shopify has developed a large number of apps that expands the capabilities of your Shopify store. These plugins and extensions enable you to pick the ones that best fit your specific needs for your Shopify store. With over 1,500 apps to choose from, both paid and free you can perform tasks such as checking stock availability and reporting, perform customer service and connect much easier with social media. All these tools and apps focus on increasing your sales and potential customer base and enhancing your online visibility.

Community

Problems crop up in business, even with the best support, or you have issues you are not sure how to handle. The Shopify community forum is a great place to ask questions, raise concerns, or get advice from people around the world who use Shopify.

Language Support

The Shopify platform supports all languages and this is an important feature. You can use the language of your choice for your store, your checkout, and all your email communication with clients.

Oberlo Takes Shopify to the Next Level

When Shopify acquired the Oberlo app in 2017, it shook up the whole world of e-commerce and all Shopify sellers gained huge benefits. With Oberlo, you connect to Aliexpress, the biggest online retail platform in China and the far East.

The Oberlo app is for the exclusive use of sellers on Shopify, it does not work with the other online retail platforms.

The Main Features Oberlo Provides to Users

Customization

Extensive changes can be made to your products descriptions, you can change or add images and change your product titles.

ePacket Filter

This filter allows you to choose items that have the fastest delivery times and only import those specific items.

Wish Lists

You can create multiple wish lists for Aliexpress products, and you do not have to change over to import the wish list products – you can import these directly from your wish lists.

Sales Tracking Dashboard

With the sales tracking dashboard you keep track of your costs, earnings, and sales.

Multiple User Accounts

This feature gives you flexibility as it allows people other than yourself to manage your online store.

Existing Products Can Be Connected

If you are already selling products from Aliexpress you can connect these to Oberlo.

Automation for Pricing

The ability to create pricing rules so that you can do bulk product pricing instead of individual pricing.

Tracking of Shipments

With the integrated order tracking, you can check up at all times on your orders.

Switch Suppliers

You can change from one supplier to another easily to take advantage of the best prices available.

Pricing and Plans

All new clients start off with a 30-day free trial of the Pro Plan with all the main features of the app without the need to provide credit card details. Billing only starts once the trial period has expired.

Starter Plan

This plan is free of charge with the following stipulations and features:

- Maximum sale of 500 products.
- Maximum of 50 orders monthly.
- Customer orders are automatically fulfilled.
- Daily sync of your products.
- Sales reports.
- Automatic pricing.
- You have access to the Oberlo Supply marketplace.
- The free Oberlo Chrome extension.

Basic Plan

Fixed monthly price with the following features and stipulations:

- You can set up 10,000 products.

- Maximum of 500 orders each month.
- All the features of the starter plan.
- Monitoring of fulfillment.
- Tracking of shipments.

Pro Plan

- Sale of up to 30,000 products.
- Unlimited orders.
- All the features of the basic plan.
- Different stores with multiple users.

Benefits of Using the Oberlo App

- Access to the extensive list of Oberlo dropshipping suppliers that have a proven track record.
- Secure, fast, and easy import from Aliexpress.
- High tech dashboard with a user-friendly interface to manage products.
- Products can be customized.
- Automated fulfillment of orders.
- Tremendous time and labour saving.
- Extra scalability.
- Video tutorials and the Oberlo blog to assist and guide users.

- One-step integration with your store on Shopify.
- Your inventory and prices are updated automatically.
- Pricing markups.
- You have access to Oberlo supply marketplace.
- Sales and shipment tracking.
- ePacket filter.
- Although only Aliexpress is supported, you can integrate Oberlo with your store on Amazon.
- Free Google Chrome extension tool that simplifies the process of importing products and managing orders.
- Ability to change product suppliers quickly and easily.

Disadvantages of Using Oberlo

- Oberlo was designed to work only with Shopify. It does not work on other standalone websites or other online retail platforms.
- Only Aliexpress is supported.
- Product editing does not take place inside Oberlo; you are redirected to your Shopify product description page.

Drawbacks of Using Shopify

Shotify has an abundance of benefits, but as with any other online retail platform, it does have drawbacks that all dropshipping business should be aware of when they choose this platform.

CMS Limitations

As a dropshipping business, your main focus is e-commerce sales and want to use a platform that gives you great flexibility, yet be easy and simplistic to operate. The Shopify CMS is not in the same league as, for instance, Wordpress; that is a major management system.

Shopify's content management system focuses on running an e-commerce store and for your needs as a dropshipping business you will have to use a bespoke theme with customization options plus the Shopify blogging platform. Solving the SMS limitations is possible with adaptations.

Content limitations

There is only the option of two different types of content in the form of a page or a blog post. This is problematic when you want to link posts to certain of your products and it is not easy to generate any additional text fields for any of the products that you offer for sale.

Product Searches

The entry level Shopify plans have very poor search capabilities with no provision for advanced search filtering. To gain access to the more advanced search features, you will have to upgrade your Shopify plan.

Payments

Shopify discourages the use of payment gateways other than their own Shopify Payment. Should you make use of any of the other payment gateways Shopify levies a 2% transaction fee for each transaction processed through any alternative gateway.

Expenses

No online retail portal give their services for free. When you join Shopify, you must examine the different fees they charge to make an informed decision of what payment plan you can afford and will suit your business needs the best.

Shopify gives you a 14-day period to try out the platform free of charge, so you can familiarize yourself with how it works and get a better idea of what your specific business needs are.

After your 14-day trial period you must choose a subscription plan to continue using the online retail portal. The plus is that they do offer discounts for annual and the two-year subscription plans. Each of the payment plans come with specific perks, with more features added to the higher-priced options.

Currently there are five different options available:

- Shopify Lite.
- Basic Shopify.
- Shopify.
- Advanced Shopify.
- Shopify Plus (this plan has negotiable fees).

Scalability

Most dropshipping companies start out small with the aim to scale as resources and finances grow. When you get to the stage where you want to expand, it is no simple or easy job to export everything you have done on Shopify because all content you have uploaded, as well as any features you have customized, is hosted by Shopify.

The search engine ranking that you have built up cannot be exported to your new site. Your new site will have to start from scratch and be indexed and start building up it's search ranking again.

It is not impossible to export data to your new site, but it will take a lot of work for you to export your customer and sales data and very time consuming.

The solution to the Shopify scalability problem is to create your own website when you start out with your dropshipping company and not rely solely on a retail platform. It is more work initially, but the benefits in the long run are worth it. Use the platform and slowly build your website along with this so that when you have to scale you already started your own website on a strong foundation with a CMS that gives you all the features of a major content managing system.

Underage Entrepreneurs

You must be 18 years or older to open your own Shopify account. This is not a huge drawback, simply a fact that very young entrepreneurs should be aware of. If you are under the age of 18, your parents or guardian must open your Shopify account on your behalf and then you will be all set to go.

Chapter 9: eBay

eBay is the biggest online auction retail platform in the e-commerce marketplace today. They cater to the needs of sellers who are first timers, occasional sellers, major and bulk sellers, and dropshipping businesses.

eBay Policies for Dropshipping

- Dropshipping is allowed on eBay providing that the dropshipping business sources his own manufacturers, wholesalers, and suppliers.
- eBay does not allow you to list products on eBay that come from any other platform or marketplace or retailer that ships products directly to your customers, meaning eBay does not allow arbitrage dropshipping.
- The dropshipping seller must guarantee that delivery from his supplier will take place within 30 days from the date that the listing ends.
- eBay holds the dropshipping business responsible for his customer satisfaction with items purchased and

the safe delivery of purchases in accordance with the timeframe listed.
- Should the dropshipping business not adhere to eBay policies, punitive measures will be instituted against the dropshipping business that include the following:
   - Cancellation of listings.
   - Administrative ending of listings.
   - Listings will be demoted or hidden from search results.
   - Seller's ratings may be lowered.
   - Buying or selling restrictions may be implemented.
   - Seller or buyer protection will be removed.
   - Suspension of the account of the dropshipping business.
   - All fees will be forfeited, both paid and payable in regards to accounts and listings that eBay has taken action against.
   - Once action has been taken against your account, no fees will be refunded or credited to you.

Work Smart and Succeed at eBay Dropshipping

To be successful with dropshipping on eBay, you must be competitive as dropshipping profit margins are low. Your aim is to sell as much as possible, but more selling means more work for you to list, process orders through your supplier, and ensure delivery of each sale one by one.

Streamline

The best way to streamline your eBay workload is to find products within your chosen niche that you can list on eBay as bulk listing or listings with variations. This lowers your workload drastically as you list these products only once. If you are unsure of how to use these listings, you can access all the information you need in their help section. You can easily minimize time spent on re-listing your products by adjusting the listing period.

Availability

Out of stock and discontinued products are a dropshipping business's nightmare. Your business cannot afford a string of negative reviews from disgruntled customers and a high volume of complaints do not go unnoticed by eBay and this could jeopardize your eBay store. eBay has very strict rules regarding and will terminate your account if you get too many customer complaints.

To prevent any of this is not difficult. You have to be on top of your game and get daily stock updates from your suppliers. Regularly check stock movements of the products you order from your suppliers and take note when stocks get low.

Your reputation as a reliable seller means everything and there is simply too much competition in e-commerce for you to neglect this most important aspect of your business.

Customer Demographics

Your success on eBay depends on many factors. It is like building a puzzle. Each piece of the puzzle has its place and must fit perfectly. The demographics of your customers play an important role in this.

Build a profile of the people that would be interested in buying the specific products that you offer. Their age group is also important as this will most likely determine their daily routines are like. These demographics will give you a good idea of what time of the day and even which days they are most likely to do their shopping on eBay. This will allow you to adjust the times and days you do your product listings.

Timing Is Key

The time of day, the day of the week and also the day of the month are all important factors for listing your products to attract the most customers. The aim is to attract as many customers as possible, make the sale as fast as you can, and maximize your profits.

Peak hours obviously attract the most potential customers and for many dropshipping companies this is the way to go. This is both a benefit and a drawback for several reasons.

- Everyone wants to list during peak hours, so you will have much more competition than during off peak traffic hours.
- Because of the sheer volume of people active on eBay during these hours, you may find that the site operates much slower than usual and this can be a huge problem near the time that an auction closes. People jump around eBay stores, looking for the best prices and products and as the site is slow, you can

lose out on sales as customers might not get to your listings in time before the auction ends.

Your customer demographics will help you greatly to avoid overwhelming numbers of competitors and the peak hour rush if you have done your demographic research into when your customers will be most likely to browse eBay.

For greater success, you need to balance the potential income during peak hours and the time schedules of your target group. It all depends on what your niche products are and whether your target group falls into the average shopper group that will be shopping when just about everyone else is shopping, or whether they will prefer other time slots to do their online purchases.

Customer Relations

At the heart of any business is the customer, and your goal for your dropshipping business is not only to attract customers but also have them come back and place more orders. It cannot be stressed enough how important it is to build good relationships with your customers.

Key to building positive relations is to gain a reputation for reliability. Customers must be able to rely on being able to get the products that you have listed and that you will make sure they get the parcels quickly and that it will arrive in excellent condition.

Should a problem pop up, your customers must know that you stand behind them and will move mountains to make sure that you find solutions and that they will be happy with the results. No matter how stressful a problem situation is for you, you cannot afford to ever be abrupt with customers, even when they are being totally unreasonable and shouting empty threats at you.

Price Control

People want the best possible price for whatever they are shopping for and will hunt around for the best bargains. This could be a logistical headache for dropshipping companies as you have to cope with all the various fees, subscription costs and the prices charged by your suppliers. To be able to make a profit, keep customers happy, and run your business effectively, you need to be aware of how your prices are affected by these four basic variables:

- Supplier prices are fixed.
- Final sales prices fluctuate.
- eBay charges: listing fees and final sale price percentages.

To effectively control prices and still make the best profit possible, you should implement the following strategies and use options to your best advantage.

- Use the Buy it Now listing option. You offer your listed items at a fixed price, the benefit is that you then make the profit you aimed for.
- Buy it Now offers a fixed insertion fee that applies to multiple as well as individual listings. The fixed insertion fee is usually lower than other listing fees.
- Setting a reserve price on a listing is another way to control pricing. The reserve price is the lowest bid that you will accept from customers on that specific item on auction.
- When using the reserve price option you must make sure not to forget to adjust your reserve price to accommodate the fact that final value fees and insertion fees varies. The drawback of using reserved pricing is that your customers cannot see what the

reserve price is and this can be very annoying for your customers.
- eBay offers a free calculator to assist you in calculating your various applicable eBay fees. This is a very helpful tool to save time and lessen stress when having to calculate all the fees and costs involved with trading on eBay.
- To have more control over your profit margin, you can opt for setting a higher starting bid in order for you to cover the fixed costs that you have no control over. These include your eBay listing fees and final value fees, as well as supplier costs and all applicable taxes and shipping costs.

Product Fulfillment

Keeping track of the whole fulfillment process is critical as you are competing with countless sellers daily on eBay. If your customers are unhappy, they will very quickly go and find what they are looking for from another seller and your reputation will soon be in shreds.

The fulfillment process can be frustrating for any dropshipping business as you do not physically handle the products, you fully rely on your suppliers to accomplish fulfillment smoothly and fast.

You want to source and retain suppliers that have their finger on the pulse of their business and will keep you up to date during the fulfillment process and immediately contact you to inform you should there be a problem or the possibility of delays. This will allow you to communicate with your customer before a situation gets out of hand.

Benefits of eBay Dropshipping

Ease of Operation

eBay is easy for anyone to negotiable with basic computer skills. It is set up to assist you in creating your store in minimum time and simple to use in operating your store. You have access to numerous plugins and tools to assist you.

Visibility

eBay is an incredibly popular online auction platform with a never ending stream of visitors looking to purchase every possible item across the broadest spectrum. This gives your eBay dropshipping business the very high visibility you need to attract as many potential customers possible in your niche.

Effort: Work Smart, Not More

Due to the huge number of daily visitors on eBay that can view your listings, you have the potential of making sales with less effort and at the best possible prices.

Technical Skills Not Required

You do not need any technical skills whatsoever to set up and operate your eBay store. Everything is put in place for you and you just have to concentrate on sourcing and listing your products.

Marketing

The very large audience that your business has access to means you do not have to spend money on intensive marketing or invest in paid traffic and SEO. This is important especially when you are starting out in the dropshipping business model.

Fraud Evaluation System

The evaluation system that eBay has put in place helps the seller and the buyer. On completion of each sale both the customer and the seller have the opportunity to evaluate the experience, give a positive, neutral or negative rating and leave a comment about the specific sale, this helps in fraud prevention.

The evaluation system helps to alert you as the seller when customers leave out of the ordinary negative evaluations. You then have the option to reject the sale and have the option to explain the reasons why the sale was rejected. Please note though that this applies to out of the ordinary circumstances only. The seller may not leave negative observations under normal circumstances; the only options the seller is allowed is to give praise and a review.

PayPal

eBay has integrated Paypal, and this enables you to accept real-time payments and this provides the seller much needed protection.

Ratings

Your rating on eBay tells potential customers what your eBay credit rating is. eBay uses three rating levels to evaluate all sellers. The ratings are based on the quality of the service you provide and your sales history. The evaluation ratings are done each month, and in e-commerce, the rating system can bring more customers or if your rating is very poor, it will have a very negative impact on your business.

Top Rated

This rating shows all potential customers that you have reached the minimum sales target that is required for this rating. This rating also makes you eligible for Top Rated Plus listing benefits on condition that you maintain the listing prerequisites.

Above Standard

You have met the minimum eBay standards required of all sellers and your customer service is acceptable.

Below Standard

You have failed to reach one or more of the minimum standards set by eBay for for customer service. A below standard rating may result in eBay taking punitive measures by dropping your listings to a lower down in the eBay search results.

Drawbacks of eBay Dropshipping

Fees

There are several different fees payable when you have an eBay store. When you use an online platform to sell you incur fees that would not be applicable if you only sold your products through your own website. The profit margin on online platforms are lower due to competition, making paying listing fees an added expense. If you sell products with add-ons, the fees will go up with each extra add-on you choose.

Customization

You have no options for customization of your store to make you memorable to customers. Everything is standardized with no options to inspire loyalty in customers through targeted product or niche marketing or innovative sales techniques.

Niche Competition

Should your chosen niche products be popular, in general, you will have fierce competition from other sellers on eBay with the same niche products and this could lead to a price war between competing sellers.

Customer Payments

Problems with non-payment by customers is a recurring problem on eBay as errors at check out crops up frequently.

Monitoring

You must regularly monitor your listings if you want to be able to sell the volume of products to make it viable to set up a dropshipping store on eBay. To make this task easier, there are several tools available to assist you in the task of monitoring your listings.

Unfair Reviews

Customers are not always nice and grumpy people often leave angry, negative reviews that are totally unfair. This is a problem for any business, but eBay does not remove reviews, whether they are unfair or out of context to what problems may have occurred. They will only remove a review under exceptional circumstances. This creates a permanent record on your account and if too many negative reviews are left, you face the possibility of your account being canceled.

Chapter 10: Amazon

Amazon is the biggest online retail platform in the world. Everyone knows about Amazon and what they do. When you become part of the Amazon brand by setting up your dropshipping store, you immediately become associated with the Amazon brand. This in itself brings huge benefits for your dropshipping company, without taking into consideration all the other benefits that dropshipping on Amazon gives you.

Using the Amazon retail platform for your dropshipping business works in more than one way, which we will detail separately and explain how each for of dropshipping works.

Amazon Dropshipping Policy

You can use Amazon FBA for your dropshipping, and basically, Amazon becomes your dropshipper as the products are shipped from an Amazon warehouse. You may also use other third-party suppliers, but you must adhere at all times to the dropshipping policy as laid down by

Amazon. Should you not adhere to the policy rules, you will face punitive measures.

- You must at all times be the seller of record for all products that you sell on Amazon.
- You must be identified as the seller of the products on all packing slips and waybills, as well as on any other information provided regarding the product or included with the product.
- You are held responsible and liable to accept and process all products returned by your customers.
- Must be in compliance at all times with all other Amazon policies and selling agreement.
- You may not buy products from any other online retailer and then have them to deliver directly to your customers.
- You are not permitted to send out any information other than your own on invoices, shipping orders, or packing slips. All information indicating seller name and contact details must be yours and not that of another company.
- Your account may be suspended and all your selling privileges revoked should you fail to comply fully with this dropshipping policy.

Dropshipping Tools

There is a large number of dropshipping tools that are compatible with the Amazon platform. This can be very confusing for entrepreneurs starting their own dropshipping business. As you gain experience, you can look into the many tools available. The following are the tools you need from the start to enable you to do so much more to grow your dropshipping business and make it worthwhile to invest in.

Feedback Express

To boost sales and grow your dropshipping business, you need as much positive feedback from customers as possible. Feedback Express helps to boost your positive reviews and remove negative feedback. This is the best way to maintain high ratings for your store and the products that you sell. Another function of Feedback Express is that it enables you to blacklist customers who behaves unethically by leaving unwarranted bad reviews.

All Amazon sellers aspire to win the Buy Box as this is a huge boost to sales and the metrics used to determine who wins the Buy Box are your feedback score and your seller rating.

This tool also sends alerts to your smart phone whenever a negative review is left on your store about your service or products.

To make things even easier for you, this tool comes with personalized email templates with an auto insert function for images, logos, links, and order information.

When you start out with FeedBack Express, you have a 30-day free trial with the option to buy at the end of your trial period.

FeedCheck

FeedCheck brings together all your product reviews so that you can see it all in one place. This is a good tool to use if you have multiple listings and enables you to see exactly how all your listings are doing and alerts you to enhance your customer service to ramp up your ratings. You can monitor the products of your competitors with this tool as well.

There are three package options to choose from.

- Startup. This is for the new business owner just starting out as an Amazon reseller. This option offers a free seven-day trial period.
- Growing Brand. This is the best option for a business with a low number of products to sell that is available from many other sellers. You have a free trial period of seven days with the option to buy.
- Enterprise. This option is more suitable for consumer goods corporations, agencies, and large brands. This package has custom pricing options calculated on number of products, unlimited store channels, and client-specific needs.

Merchant Words

The Merchant Words app collects data from the Amazon autocomplete search bar about what words and phrases Amazon users use while searching for products. The data is used to identify high ranking keywords and product trends.

There is the silver, gold, and platinum subscription options to choose from.

The app has the following features:

- Amazon regional, per country and global data.
- Monthly searches.
- Seasonality of keywords.
- Keyword collections.
- Keyword search volumes.
- Pge One analysis.
- ASIN plus.
- Keyword history.
- Multiple users.
- Digital shelf dashboard.
- Keyword multiplier.
- Performance metrics.

Amazon Volume Listing Tools

There are several tools developed by Amazon to assist you to easily manage inventory and order information with downloadable spreadsheets. Listing tools are available to quickly change and modify product quantities and product pricing.

Sellery

This is a repricing tool for Amazon that works in real-time to adapt to marketing conditions using a large number of price combinations for a personalized pricing strategy for your Amazon store. Constant monitoring is through smart filters that react immediately to changes to keep you competitive.

Pricing starts at 1% of your monthly sales with the minimum charge of $50 and the maximum is $150 monthly. The product comes with a 14-day trial period.

Features include:

- Scheduled repricing.
- Real-time repricing.
- Automatic pricing rules.
- Solutions for private labeling.
- Pricing strategies that can be customized to suit client needs.
- Net margin management.
- Support from Amazon experts.
- All the features enhance your chance to win the sought after Buy Box.

Shopify

Shopify announced integration with Amazon in 2017. This means your Amazon store can now be added to Shopify as a sales channel on your Shopify store. It takes only a few minutes to sync your Shopify products with your products listed on Amazon. Shopify will send you alerts if you have sales on Amazon that must be fulfilled. This integration opens up vast new sales opportunities to grow your dropshipping business.

Add a Product Tool

This interactive tool is used to small numbers of products by adding each product one at a time, as opposed to using bulk listing. This web-based interface is ideal for the following tasks:

- To create a new listing for a product that does not exist on Amazon. When you list a new product not yet for sale on Amazon, they then create a product detail page for this.

- To match to an existing product listing. You must match the product you want to sell to the existing product detail page.

Product Approvals and Restrictions

Before you open your store on Amazon you need to make sure in which category the products fall that you want to sell. It is vitally important that you go through the restricted products help pages on the official Amazon website. Amazon is very strict about the policies governing all products offered for sale on their online retail platform.

Before you start your store on Amazon or when you want to bring new products into your store, you need to make absolutely sure in which category the products fall and what policies and laws you must adhere to. The consequences of not adhering to these policies have dire consequences that could result in your account being canceled and you could be banned from using Amazon in the future.

Broadly, products on Amazon fall into three categories.

- Products eligible with no need for approval.

- Restricted products that need approval, with some products that need state- or country-related approval as well as approval according to Amazon's own policies.
- Prohibited products that will not be approved to be listed on Amazon at all.

The onus rests upon you as the seller to make sure all your listings are in order and absolutely worth the time spent to do this. You worked hard to start your dropshipping business and deserve to reap all the benefits, and there is no need for your business venture to fail because of rules and regulations.

Seller Fees

Fees are a drawback every seller face, no matter what online retail platform you choose. Knowing exactly what seller fees you have to deal with and how the fees differ between selling plans enables you to decide which selling plan is the best suitable one for your business that will minimize the impact it has on your profit.

Please note that all selling fees discussed here are applicable to selling in the USA. Should you operate your dropshipping business from another country, you need to confirm what fees are applicable to that specific country.

You have the choice of the professional seller plan and the individual seller plan and fees differ for each plan.

Per-Item Fees

This fee is applicable on every item you sell on Amazon. Take note, the per item fee is not levied if you use the professional seller plan.

Amazon collects the full amount that the customer paid when you make a sale. This includes shipping fees, per-item fee, any add-ons such as gift wrap, and the charge for any other extras the customer had asked for.

Referral Fees

A referral fee is paid on every item sold. Several product categories have a predetermined minimum referral fee per item. When a product you sold falls in the minimum referral fee category, you are liable for either the referral fee or the per-item fee, depending on which of these are the greater.

Shipping Fees

When orders are not fulfilled by Amazon, professional sellers are liable for shipping fees on media products. Individual sellers are liable for shipping fees on all products sold. The shipping fees are calculated according to the category of the item and the charges set for that specific category, as well as the charge for whichever shipping service chosen by the customer. These shipping charges are passed on to you as the seller.

When you make use of the Amazon FBA system, you will be charged FBA fees that include storage, fulfillment, and optional extras services. This shipping fee is levied in addition to the fees payable for selling on Amazon.

Variable Closing Fees

This fee is charged on all media item for both professional and individual sellers. The fee is calculated according to predetermined fees for each category.

Professional Seller Plan

- A monthly subscription fee.
- Referral fee that varies as per category on every item sold.
- Variable closing fees that are category specific.
- The Amazon marketplace per item fee is not applicable on this seller plan.
- Shipping fees only applicable on media products (DVD, video, video games, software, music, and books).
- Plan for selling in excess of 40 items per month.

Individual Seller Plan

- No monthly subscription fee on this plan.
- Per item fee applicable on each item sold.
- Referral fees.
- Variable closing fees.
- Shipping fees applicable for all items sold.
- This plan is for selling less than 40 items per month.

Amazon Fulfillment Service

In 2006, Amazon launched the FBA (Fulfilled by Amazon) dropshipping model. The FBA model works in more than one way.

You, as the seller, ship your bulk purchases (minimum size orders from suppliers) to an Amazon warehouse where it is stored and from where it is shipped to your individual customers as they put orders in and Amazon takes care of the packaging and shipping.

Dropshipping companies also use the FBA service for products sold in their Amazon store and Amazon takes care of the fulfillment.

You can also make use of the FBA service to fulfill your orders that you sell on other online retail platforms, as well as products sold through your own website. You combine your fulfillment from all the different stores you operate under the Amazon fulfillment umbrella.

The Amazon FBA moves the goalposts for the dropshipping business model as this is no longer dropshipping directly from your supplier to your customer. You have to purchase some inventory, even if it is the minimum order size determined by your supplier and that must be stored in an Amazon warehouse.

Benefits of Using FBA

Reliable and Swift Processing

Amazon is the largest retail platform and has a proven track record as being the best globally for delivering a product to its destination the fastest and in perfect condition with no mishaps.

Better Margins

Most of the times your suppliers will offer you wholesale prices when you purchase products to go into storage at Amazon, which is a saving from the prices suppliers offer to you when you place individual orders with them.

Benefits Specific to Amazon FBA

Amazon offers incentives to encourage to list your products directly on Amazon for dropshipping.

Eligibility for the following features can push your conversion rate up:

- Super Saver Shipping.
- Amazon Prime.
- Buy Box.

- Amazon handles product returns on your behalf by communicating directly with the customers and shipping a replacement item to the client on your behalf.

Drawbacks

Storage Fees

You have to pay for the storage of your inventory at an Amazon warehouse. Dropshipping businesses usually only store their best selling products for use of the FBA as it is not cost-effective for products with lower demand. Your suppliers do not charge you for storage, as the products still belong to them until you place an order.

FBA Fees

Fees are charged for the use of the FBA service, and this lowers your profit margin.

Long-Term Storage Fees

You are liable for the long-term storage fees on products that have been in storage longer than a year. This fee is applicable over and above the normal storage fees payable.

The long-term storage fee is calculated on per-cubic-foot and per unit, and the long terms storage fee applicable will be whichever of these two measurement costs are the highest.

No Dedicated Storage

There is no dedicated storage space allocated to your inventory stored in the warehouse. Products from all suppliers are sorted into categories at Amazon so your inventory will be placed in storage together with the same products from numerous suppliers. When it comes to shipping the product to your client, it may not be the item you bought from your supplier; it could be from any supplier.

To prevent your items being mixed up with the same product from elsewhere, you could have an SKU-level sticker attached to your specific items which come at a cost of $0.02 per item to be labeled. This may seem like a needless extravagance, but this way you ensure that your customer gets the exact item you bought from your supplier and not an item that falls under the same item name, but might not be of the same quality as your originally purchased item.

Benefits of Dropshipping on Amazon

- You gain the immediate advantages of access to the buying audience of the largest online retail platform locally and globally.
- The Fulfillment by Amazon system with all the benefits as detailed in the section titled Amazon Fulfillment Service.
- Amazon ads lowers advertising costs as you can control how much you spend as Amazon does not stipulated a minimum amount you must spend to make use of their ads.
- Less overhead expenses to run your business.
- Automation for processing orders, delivery and marketing.
- Tools for repricing products are available, saving the need to update manually.
- Buy Box for achieving ratings of excellent.

Disadvantage of Dropshipping on Amazon

- Listing fees.
- Warehouse storage fees if you use Amazon FBA.
- Extra warehouse storing fees for long-term storage should items be stored longer than 365 days.

- Vulnerability of your sales data as Amazon has access to all data relating to running of your store. This includes the overall totals of your sales and which of your items are your top sellers.
- Customization is very limited as Amazon controls all aspects of your marketing, and branding you use.
- The dropshipping policy places very strict boundaries of what a dropshipping business may do and what not.
- Punitive measures should you fail in adhering to any of their policies.

Chapter 11: Your Own Dropshipping Website

The dropshipping business model is incredibly flexible with all the online retail platforms available to choose from and the apps and plugins everyone has access to. This makes it quick and easy to start your dropshipping business. All the benefits you get when selling on the retail platforms, from their templates, specialized apps, and marketing, many new entrepreneurs are happy to only use these platforms. It is simple and easy and you make money. This is all great and all dropshipping companies should make use of these available online retail platforms.

Why Is It Important to Create a Website?

This is the first question most people ask as it seems a lot of unnecessary work for very low returns. There are several reasons why it is important that while you use the online retail platforms, you start building your own business website.

Your own website gives your business legitimacy in the eyes of potential customers and suppliers and wholesalers you want to work with. It changes from the perception of you just being a listing on a platform or a disembodied store amongst thousands of other online stores to be found on the retail platforms.

Manufacturers and suppliers like working with dropshipping business that have an established website. Even though you are only starting out and have a very small customer base, it shows your suppliers that you are serious about being in business and not just another fly-by-night dropshipping business out to make a few quick bucks and then close up shop and move on. When you approach new suppliers, they will check online to see if you have a website; you build trust and rapport with suppliers through your website.

Another important reason to establish your own website is your competitors. Dropshipping companies that want to be visible and successful have their own e-commerce websites. One of the key analytics of e-commerce is competitor analysis and not having your own website can have an adverse effect on the success of your business.

Setting Everything in Motion

Not everyone is technology savvy and setting up your own website is not something everyone tackles with enthusiasm. You need an e-commerce dropshipping specific website design that incorporates as many features as possible to make running your website easy and allow clients to navigate through your website without stumbling blocks created by bad website design.

You have the choice of having your website designed by professionals according to your specific criteria. You can opt to search to find the correct templates and designs through an internet search. There is an abundance of good website creating templates to choose from that will suit your niche and features that address all the specifics you need and want for your own website.

Your budget is the determining factor for setting up your website, but most of the templates available will have free options. These free templates are more basic, but usable if you are strapped for cash.

To start, you need to set in place your website hosting, with WordPress website hosting being the top choice from users with dropshipping extensions and plugins. Choose design templates and select an appropriate domain name.

Website Hosting

Choosing the correct and most beneficial web hosting service for your dropshipping business website is of the utmost importance. This can be very confusing when you are starting out to have to keep everything in mind of what type of hosting is best and what to look for in a web hosting solution. Often, people just throw up their hands and go with the first web hosting they come across when doing a search, just to not have to worry about this aspect anymore. Some of the aspects to check might sound technical but are manageable with tools and taking some time to work through this all. To guide you to making the right decision, we highlight the most important features you must check when choosing your web hosting solution.

Reviews

To start, do research on the web hosting services you are interested in. Sadly, often the websites that proclaim they publish factual reviews lets you down as web hosting services do not like negative reviews about their companies so they do anything possible to remove these reviews from the sites they appear on. Do a Google search by typing in the name of the company you want to find out about and the word reviews and you will get fast and accurate reviews from websites that publish not-paid-for reviews and from information published on the personal blogs of people who have used the specific hosting service.

Bandwidth and Storage Limits

A dropshipping businesses need a sufficient storage limit to enable you to run your dropshipping business as you will be offering products from different suppliers. Your hosting service must be able to guarantee the upload of a minimum of 10,000 products with ease and no problems.

Bandwidth is very important, so make sure you find out whether the hosting service has limitations on bandwidth or whether it is unlimited. When customers browse your store, they will download information and should your hosting service have limitations this will cause problems and customers will become impatient if they are unable to download information and images.

PHP 7 Support And SSL Certificates

One of the search engine ranking factors is whether sites have SSL certificates installed or not. Sites with SSL certificates have better ranking. When customers browse and they get a Google popup warning that a specific website does not have any SSL certification. This warns the person browsing and most will close down that site and move to a site that they feel they can trust.

Make sure that the web hosting service you choose supports PHP 7, the latest version of

PHP that is available. This is most important for your dropshipping website as some of the top dropshipping plugins have stopped supporting all the earlier versions of PHP.

Pricing

Web hosting services can be very costly, especially for a startup e-commerce business. Cloud hosting offers great cost-saving advantages of unlimited bandwidth with automatic scaling that automatically adjusts when your website deals with an increase in traffic.

Performance

The performance of a hosting service can be measured with the available tools to check on how fast or how slow loading times are and the actual page speed. Another option is to visit websites that are clients of a specific hosting service and experience the loading times. This will help you to eliminate hosting services that give poor performance.

Security

The majority of hosting solutions today provide users with cPanel website management. Check whether the hosting service use cPanel or another lesser known managing system. You need a secure control panel that prevents all back-door entries, plus offers secure access through SSH and FTP.

E-Commerce Platform Support

Your hosting service must support the top e-commerce online platforms through one-click installation.

Customer Service

A reliable hosting service will have 24/7 customer support plus phone support. The success of your business depends on prospective customers being able to visit your website at any time with minimal interruptions of service.

Scaling Ability

If the hosting service you are interested in does not offer automatic scaling, it would be wise to choose a service that does or make absolutely sure their servers can upscale to meet your needs. Your business cannot afford to lose customers and lower order placement through the inability of the servers to keep up.

Your Own Domain Name

Your domain name is your address and unique. All computers on the internet have an identifying numeric IP address, but people will never remember specific IP address amongst the billions of IP addresses on the net. Domain names were created when it was realized that having an IP address was simply not enough for finding specific websites. So coupling a unique IP address with a unique domain name creates your one-of-a-kind address. No business can afford to disappear in cyberspace; when people cannot find you, they will search for another business that offers what you do.

Having your own domain name is not a matter of simply helping the search engines find your website, it has other benefits many people do not think about.

Internet Mobility

Once you have created your unique domain name, it belongs to you. Should you decide to transfer from your web host or change your server, you take your domain name with you. Not owning your domain name creates huge problems for you. You will have to start over again with a different URL and you lose all the effort you have put into building your brand name.

Credibility

Without a domain name, you are allocated a generic from the web host company or ISP. This clearly shows on your web address and points to your business not being very professional and trustworthy. E-commerce has taken over the world, but humans are not the most trusting creatures. The onus is on you to give them reasons to trust you and to want to do business with you. Having a free generic URL tells people you are not prepared to spend money on your online presence through registering a domain name. No small business can afford to get labeled as cheap; potential customers would turn to other companies that show they are serious about their business.

Shows That You Are Proactive

Your domain name shows that you are keeping up-to-date with the changes in technology. The younger generations are very tech-savvy and pick up on the finer details, and you do not want to alienate a huge portion of your potential customer base by saving money by using generic URLs.

Choose a Domain Name That Fits

You do not only have to choose a domain name that is your company name. If you choose a domain name that matches what your business is all about, a word that connects searchers online to your niche, it draws in people searching for anything in your niche.

Essentials for an E-Commerce Website

You want your website to reflect your products and your niche and create a shopping experience for your customers that they will remember and make them come back again.

Match Products, Design and Content

You want your customers to associate your website with the products you offer and they want. Every aspect of your website must focus on your niche, from colours, text, images, videos to music. Your client demographics come into play as well; your website must appeal to the type of person who is interested in the products you offer.

User-Friendly Shopping Cart

Nothing frustrates a shopper more than when they have decided to start purchasing to then get bogged down with the website shopping cart that makes it impossible to add, change, or remove products. When they want to go back and browse some more to get stuck on not being able to continue shopping. The customer is king, so take your time and look at all the features that will make it easy and a process without stress.

Keep the Check-Out Process Simple

Your goal is to get your customers easily through the check-out process as you need the highest sales conversion possible. There are many reasons customers abandon the shopping cart before finalizing the transaction. There is a portion of shoppers who do not complete the check-out process because they were only just looking around and comparing prices. You have no control over this. What you can control has been researched and analyzed by Baymard.com and the percentages of carts abandoned for each reason is an eye-opener and clearly point out ways to make your website customer friendly and appealing.

Customers want their shopping to be easy and without frustration. Your check-out process must be easy, smooth and meet the requirements of your customers.

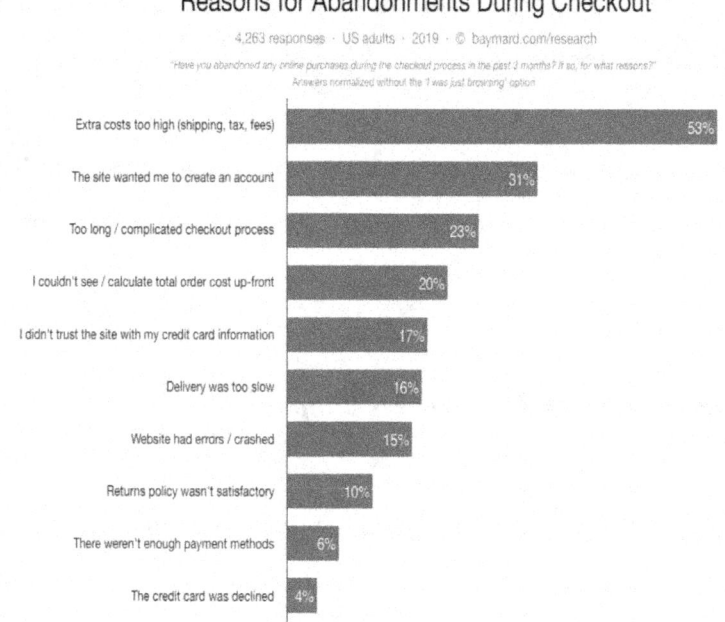

(Baymard Institute, n.d.)

Social Media

Social media has become an integral part of the lives of millions of people. It is crucial in the world of business today to make social media part of your website. Today people check social media for trends and to see what is being said about a product they might be interested in. Using social media as a marketing tool brings your products to the attention of a large number of people and leads to a much higher conversion rate in sales.

Security

Your e-commerce website for your dropshipping business must have top security features. The Payment Card Industry Data Security Standard (PCI DSS) is the information security standard that is a necessity for any website that will handle credit cards.

Security is so important to shoppers that this is usually the first thing they look for on a website, and if the website is not secure, they will leave, no matter how much they want to buy a specific product.

Making sure that your website design incorporates all the necessary security measures becomes an incentive for buyers to become regular buyers for your products through your website.

Multi-Language Support

Many entrepreneurs don't think of the major benefits they gain if they bring multi-language support into their website. This is not just a convenience tool for customers, it gives you a competitive edge over your competitors that do not have multi-language support.

Multinational corporations have embraced multi-language support, but it is still greatly neglected by smaller e-commerce. E-commerce has become such a huge part of all international buying that smaller businesses can get a head start and enjoy the benefits while their competitors are falling further behind.

This is a very productive marketing tool that opens your business up to the international markets and bring you new customers that are interested in your niche products. Being able to communicate in their own language will grab their attention immediately. When you add the top world languages, you expand your potential client base and the possibility to double your sales.

A multilingual website removes cultural barriers and earn the trust of international buyers. Often people do not feel at ease buying over the internet in a language that they do not fully understand.

Most of the major search engines are able to run searches in other languages besides English. With language support you immediately maximize the chance that your website will be picked up when people search for your products.

Plugins Are Necessities

You simply cannot run your dropshipping website without plugins. You need them to take care of the myriad tasks that would eat up your time if you had to do them manually.

The plugins you need depend on which online retail platform you have teamed up with as some of them are specific to a platform and won't work very well on other platforms.

The aim here is to introduce you to the plugins that have the best reviews with the highest ratings done by users. These are worth it to take on a trial basis and see which fit your own website and products the best.

Oberlo Dropshipping App

This app is best suited to Shopify and available in the app store on Shopify. It has super features that include listings of approved dropship suppliers, this makes looking for new suppliers incredibly easy. Since Amazon integrated with Shopify this app is used to sync your Amazon sales channel on Shopify. The app has a free option plus two paid for options. For full details of all the features that Oberlo offer please see Chapter 8, sub-paragraph Oberlo Takes Shopify to the Next Level.

Social Rabbit

This WooCommerce app is an automated tool to promote your website and business on social media.

Plugin SEO

This plugin is available in the Shopify app store. There is a free version available as well as a paid for version. The free version of Plugin SEO advise when there are any issues with how your website performs on the search engines. It also provides basic SEO techniques.

AliDropship

AliDropship is a paid for plugin and provides the Aliexpress dropshipping plugin for WordPress. This is a plugin designed for users who import products from the Aliexpress marketplace. This plugin is hugely popular as the majority of features are automated.

Alidropship Woo

This is the Alidropship plugin designed to work with WooCommerce and is a paid for plugin. This version of the plugin is more advanced as it is a newer design and provides enhanced features, making it a better option than the generic original version of the plugin.

Content Egg

This rugged plugin is designed for WordPress and very popular with users. It is designed to update your product information.

Product Reviews

This WordPress plugin is used for product reviews and has all the standard features needed for reviewing your products on offer.

Dropshix

This plugin comes in two versions. The standard option is free and the advanced features option is paid for. Dropshix tracks shipments provides auto-synchronized real-time reports. It comes with an integrated extension for Chrome.

MailChimp

MailChimp is an email marketing plugin that assists you in doing email marketing for your business. This is a valuable tool for all e-commerce businesses to send out emails in bulk to alert customers to new products available.

Integration Options

It has integration options with social media, for instance Facebook, plus access testing and scheduling to boost your open rates. No limitations on image hosting at no cost enhances your marketing.

Templates

MailChimp offers several standard templates, but you have the option to import your own templates as well. You can customize the standard templates offered as well with easy point-and-click editor without the need for coding expertise.

Logo

This plugin is offered free for a maximum of 2,000 contacts. Their logo is displayed on your subscription form and your campaign. The upgraded version of the plugin gives you the option to remove their logo from all outgoing mail from your business.

Comparative Metrics

You can track your email campaigns with an analysis of how the campaign is performing. Another feature is that you can see your metrics compare with user Mailchimp subscribers.

No program, plugin, and extension is perfect as it is impossible to design these to cater to the needs of each individual user. MailChimp addresses most functions adequately with a few drawbacks that you need to be aware of before choosing this plugin.

Websites that Are Subscription and Membership Based

The MailChimp plugin used on WordPress sites, as well as PayPal, can sometimes be problematic. Should your website have membership and subscription options, you will encounter difficulties. You also have the option to set up autoresponders, but the drawback is that the autoresponders only works when people subscribed through one of your web forms and does not work at all with any contacts that you have imported.

Templates Are Standard and Plain

The templates are very plain and not eye-catching for the readers. To make the MailChimp templates more appealing means you have to spend time modifying them or opt to import your own templates that are focussed on your customer demographics and products.

Interface Issues

It takes time for the user to become familiarized with the MailChimp interface and some users find it cumbersome. This plugin works great for a business that sends out information updates and newsletters, but if your email is high volume, this becomes time consuming.

Another interface drawback is that you are not able to send out multiple email lists at the same time. You are restricted to sending out subscriber lists one by one.

Suspension of Accounts

Should you receive complaints of spamming about your emails, or receive high numbered of unsubscribe requests, MailChimp reserves to cancel or suspend your account without notifying you of this. This means users must be vigilant and test emails before sending out to their subscribers to prevent suspension or cancellation.

Advantages of Your Own Website

Trustworthy Image

When customers come to your website they are faced with a website that has been designed to be professional and customer orientated. People are more comfortable to spend money with a company that has a professional website instead of a listing on a retail platform that is totally anonymous.

No Competition

Competition can be a headache when you have to compete with so many other listings that sell the same or very similar products. Visitors to your website see only items displayed that you sell. On the online auction platforms, prices are often driven down to such an extent that there is no profit margin left as there are simply too many sellers competing. When selling through your own website, you can set realistic prices that gives you a decent profit margin.

Fees to List and Sell Fall Away

Depending on which payment options you have on your website, there may still be certain fees to pay if you offer PayPal and similar payment options. You eliminate many other fees that erode your profit margin that come with using the online retail platforms such as fees for each product that you list, subscription fees, and more.

Disadvantages

Start-Up Costs

You will have initial costs when you start your own website, so need to budget for this. However, the initial cash outlay depends on your choice of website. If you want a custom-built website created by a web design company, your start-up costs will be high. When you choose to put some work in you are able to lower the costs greatly with a WordPress website that gives you a fully functional website with all the necessities.

Support

You do not have the advantages of the support staff you get when you subscribe to the online retail platforms. When problems crop up on your website, you will have to deal with it yourself. However, if you had chosen a reputable website builder, you will have access to their technical support team to assist you.

Traffic Builds Slowly

When you have just started up your own website, it will take time to build organic traffic. You will have to build up your client base over time and start to slowly build up loyal customers that will return to your website.

Chapter 12: Your Online Presence

The importance of establishing a strong online presence cannot be emphasized enough. A business with no online presence simply does not exist on the World Wide Web. The search engines cannot find you, no matter how great the products you sell may be. The stronger your online presence is, the easier it is for search engines to find you when people do searches for your products and your niche.

We will go through each of the strategies you should use to bring you the best online presence possible and how each strategy increases your visibility to the search engines and prospective clients.

Marketing

Marketing can be compared to an intricately woven spider web. It involves every aspect of your business and it must all come together to enhance your online presence, broaden your customer base to improve your profit margin. Many aspects and forms of marketing is detailed in the paragraphs below, so here we will focus on other important aspects of marketing not mentioned.

Demographics and Psychographics

Google Analytics is the place to start to gather information and your customer demographics, as well as psychographics. These statistics are used to focus your marketing; otherwise, your marketing will be random, hit-and-run, and not effective at all.

Demographics statistics give you information on the age groups, family background, level of education, and income as well as the location of your customers. Psychographics give you answers as to the motivation of your customers – why are they specifically interested in the products that you offer?

All these statistics allow you to build what is called a customer persona of what makes your potential customers tick. Google Analytics offer a huge range of statistics analysis and you can add more to give you the tightest possible focus for your marketing efforts.

Customer Reviews and Ratings

Adding a feedback page to your website and your online store is the best way to build trust. Humans are not very trusting, and when shopping online, they often have reason for this skepticism. Use this scepticism as a marketing tool by having a section for testimonials and ratings by customers and, most importantly, have a section where customers can leave reviews on your products and services.

Potential customers can read the reviews plus your feedback on the reviews and how you resolved any problems. This customer interaction is the fastest way to build trust and shows customers you are prepared to be completely transparent.

Marketing Trends

Look into marketing strategies that are trendy and very popular for getting your marketing message across to the widest customer base for your niche.

All the major social networks allow entrepreneurs to interact with their customers via private messaging. You can converse directly with potential customers on all the social media platforms that you subscribe to. Regularly check the private message on your social media pages and answer questions in the shortest possible timeframe. This provides a channel for both marketing and customer service.

Live chat is another marketing trent to investigate. Shopify assists users through several live chat bot options available in their extensions library. This option may not be best for a startup business that does not have the manpower available for live chat, it is an option to keep in mind for when your business has grown to accommodate this.

Chat bots is a marketing strategy that does not need manpower. The bots can answer basic questions for customers without you being there.

Display Ads

A low-cost marketing option that is very popular is display ads. Display advertising has grown and improved tremendously over the past decade. This type of advertisements are now focussed on your target audience with much better results than in the past.

Display advertising works in two ways. You go to the top websites that represent your niche and see if you can buy ad space on that website. This brings you advertising straight to the people who are interested in your niche products. The second option is to work through an established ad network that will handle your display ads and placement.

The goal of display ads is to bring your brand to the attention of potential customers that fall in your niche instead of having your display ads reach a large portion of people who are not interested in your niche products.

Be Where Your Niche Gathers Online

Search to see where the people gather on the internet that would be your niche customers. Wherever there is a niche, there will be blogs and groups on social media. Join these groups and become part of your niche. See what they discuss about your niche products and what their needs and wants are.

This is subtle marketing as you do not bombard people with your business and ads. You are an expert about your niche and can answer questions, give pointers, and advice. Most bloggers and social media groups will be happy to use input from you and include posts you make and give credit to your business.

Retarget

Statistics show that up to 98% of people do not buy when they visit a website for the first time as people love to window-shop before making any decisions. Instead of being despondent about the low conversion rate for first time visitors, see it as an opportunity for another marketing strategy. Statistics show that when you retarget customers with display ads, the potential conversion rate goes up to 70%.

Currently retarget marketing is extremely underutilized for various reasons. Some businesses feel they don't have the time to try and retarget potential customers. Many, especially entrepreneurs starting out in the dropshipping business model, simply are not aware of this marketing strategy. This means now is the perfect time for you to start using retarget marketing as it puts you ahead of your competition.

Cross Sell and Upsell

Cross-selling and upselling is one of the top marketing strategies to engage impulse buyers as this type of buyer is the easiest to convince to make more than just the one purchase they originally planned on.

As a dropshipping business, your store and website is silent. Your potential customers are not confronted with eager sales people giving helpful advice to upsell your products or to cross sell by suggesting other products that go well with their choice. You can do cross-selling by bundling groups of products together that compliment each other.

It does not matter whether you have an online store on a retail platform or whether you sell directly through your own website, there are great plugins available for cross-selling and upselling. There is a variety of plugins available for Shopify, WooCommerce, and WordPress, as well as independent plugins available for this marketing technique.

Let these plugins be the voice of your business with subtle pop ups based on the items visitors are browsing with pop ups to alert them to more products that they might be interested in.

Try out several of the upsell and cross-sell plug ins available to find which of these fit your marketing needs the best.

Costly Marketing Strategies

With all the options for low-cost and cost-effective marketing available, it is not an absolute necessity to use costly marketing strategies. If you are able financially to use high cost marketing, then there are two very popular strategies you can look at for your business.

Promotions and giveaways have always been popular with all types of businesses and you can draw a lot of attention to your dropshipping business with these tactics. It is worth it to think about this and see if you can work this into your budget.

Social media has brought about what is called influencer marketing. With the global popularity of social media, these influencers can wield a lot of power, and if any of them promote your products, it could drive sales tremendously. Should you be interested in this type of marketing, it is worth spending time researching which influencers would benefit your niche on the different social media platforms.

Branding

Branding is an important part of a dropshipping business often neglected. Some feel that having their dropshipping store on Shopify or listing on the online retail platforms is enough and give them adequate online presence.

Branding makes your store stand out from countless others. When you dropship on the retail platforms, you become invisible without branding. Yes, building your own unique brand takes effort and time, you have the choice to be faceless in the crowd, or stand out, to be remembered. Your branding on the retail platforms and branding on your own website goes hand in hand.

Creating your own brand builds trust; customers see you as trustworthy because they can identify your business with your unique brand. This works as a great marketing strategy as well.

Branding for the dropshipping model works different from branding other retail businesses as you do not physically stock the products and your suppliers handle storage and delivery.

Branding flows through your website, your online store on the retail platforms and social media. Your goal with branding it to make sure people will recognize your logo and associate it with your business in as many different places on the internet as possible. Branding gives your dropshipping a distinct and personal identity.

It is important to realize that branding must grow with your dropshipping business from the start. To try and do branding when you have more time, or you feel financially more secure does not work very well. Trying to retroactive with your branding does not work very well. You have lost too much ground as all the customers who bought from you in the past has nothing specific to remember you by and will have moved on.

Social Media Advertising

Social media was born roughly four decades ago as newsgroups where people could communicate, and we all know the huge influence social media has on just about every part of people's lives. Taking your branding to social media gives you access to a huge audience to be exploited with your branding and advertising. Make your presence known on every available social media platform with ad campaigns and your logo on everything.

Using social media as a marketing tool for branding benefits you in another way as well. Every time you post on your Instagram account or your Facebook account brings you organic traffic at a much lower cost than the more traditional forms of marketing.

Here is a short list of the benefits of using social media to improve your brand:

- Organic traffic at very low cost.
- Very little competition as the majority of businesses neglect social media marketing.
- Pictures really do speak much louder than the written word. Post videos and images that relate to your business and your niche products as this gives people a much better insight into what you are selling.
- Easy to set up accounts on social media and easy to use.
- None or very low advertising costs. Most of the social media platforms do offer paid for advertising, but this is not a necessity. You are able to successfully advertise on social media and reach a large audience. Should you at a later stage decide to

boost your branding even more, you can opt for paid for ad campaigns.

White Labeling

Everyone knows how incredibly competitive the world's marketplaces have become. White labeling is such an effective branding strategy that Amazon has pushed into white labeling and has started offering their own white-branded products to increase profits.

It is a simple concept that works very well for a dropshipping business. You negotiate with your dropshipping supplier to white label the products that you order from him with your own white label and logo instead of his own company labels. By switching labeling, the supplier rebrands the product for you and it becomes "your" product. Many dropshipping suppliers are happy to do this as they still sell their products, just with a different label. The important thing for the suppliers is that no changes are made to their products, only the label changes.

Extra Marketing Strategy with White Labeling

You can negotiate with your suppliers to enable an extra marketing strategy when they rebrand your orders to include a packing slip with your contact information, your logo, and your company policies.

Packaging and Delivery Marketing

Another option that benefit your branding is to have a brochure or mini-catalogue included to introduce customers to more products that you offer.

Blogging

Blogging is big business today and a vital part of your online presence that benefits all aspects of your dropshipping business. To fully realize the importance of having your own blog, consider that currently there are more than 409 million people monthly reading in excess of 23.7 billion pages. The graph below indicates how trustworthy internet users find information from blogs.

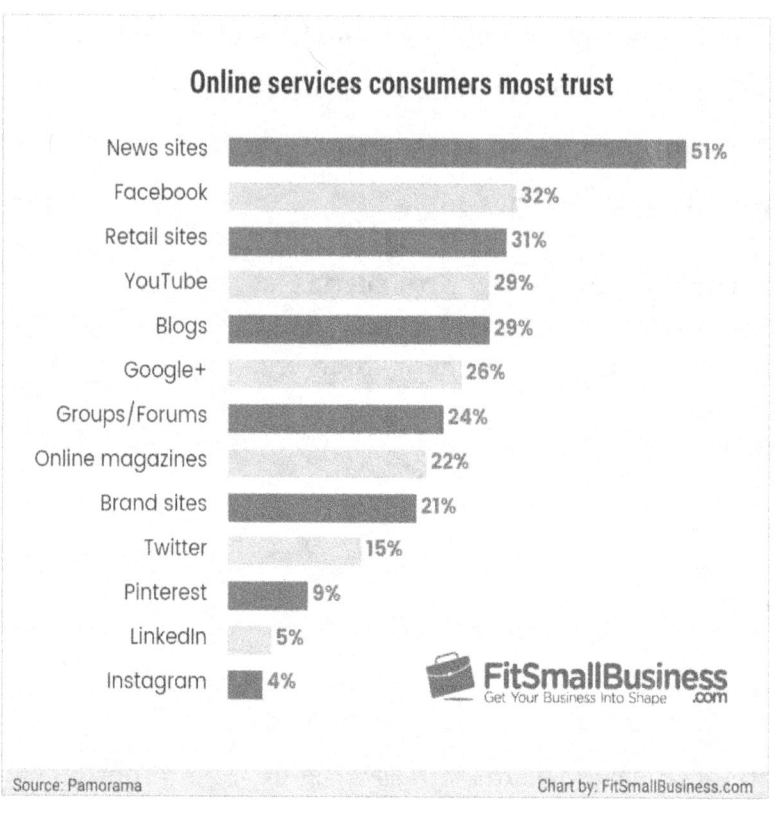

(FitSmallBusiness, 2017)

You do not have to be a world-renowned author and spend hours writing blog posts for it to be effective. Make it short and interesting, compare it to posting regularly on social media. Everyone spends time, most people do so daily, posting on the various social media platforms about everyday matters. Blogging is a business asset that helps you grow your business by simply doing what you do on Facebook and Twitter already.

The multitude of benefits of blogging fall into four categories.

SEO Benefits

Each blog post you create adds a new page to your website. This is new and unique content that has never been indexed by the search engines. With each new blog post, your ratings improve and you become more visible when searches are made using your keywords and results in more traffic to your website. One of the factors search engines look for is the freshness of the content and blogging keeps feeding the search engines.

When search engines check your website and they find only stale content, the times between checking your website become longer each time. By feeding them fresh content on a regular basis, it keeps them interested and the search engines check your website regularly at short intervals.

Keep your blog postings knowledgeable and make it interesting. Other bloggers will refer to your blog content in their own blogs and include a link to your blog post. This generates what is called authoritative links or inbound links.

This is hugely beneficial for your SEO and will increase website traffic.

When you write niche specific posts with a tight focus, it gives you the opportunity to use long-tailed keywords consisting of search phrases of several words. Blog posts concentrating on benefits of a specific product or filling a specific customer need will generate more traffic from visitors with an interest in those specific aspects of the product you offer, thus benefiting your optimization.

Your blog posts have long-term optimization benefits that stretch over weeks and months after publishing a specific blog post without having to redo that specific blog post.

Benefits for Your Brand

The dropshipping business model face stiff competition and many competitors use a shortcut by investigating what other stores in the same niche are doing and using ideas from these stores for themselves in their store design and for marketing purposes.

Use your writing skills to mention features of your own store that makes you stand out from other stores in your niche and highlight specifics about certain products you offer. Using these subtle reminders in your blog posts make you memorable to visitors and they recognise your store through your blogging. This type of blog posts cannot easily used by a competitor as they would with more generic posts.

Stores that serve a niche and sell all the products related to that niche is seen as speciality stores by prospective customers. They feel that if you specialize you are an authority on that niche and that you are a responsible seller that understands all the specific issues, needs, and wants of that community. For example, if your niche is fishing and all the equipment and gadgets specific to that niche, they feel your knowledge and input can be trusted.

Your blog posts give you the opportunity to show your customers that you are knowledgeable and part of that niche community. Well-thought-out blog posts is one of the best brand building opportunities for your business.

Marketing Benefits

To successfully use your blog to promote your business on all the social media platforms is not difficult. The rule is to give the readers high-quality content and not generic content they can find everywhere else. Post the links to your blog articles on your social media accounts and then take it a step further. Present the contents of your blog posts in different formats that are eye-catching and suitable to be used on other platforms. Infographics and informational or product educational videos are two of the most popular formats and people love sharing, especially within a niche community. This widens the audience you reach and has the potential of new customers.

Better Customer Relations

People love to learn about things they have little knowledge of, or things they want to know more about. What they do not like, is to be lectured, it makes them feel they are not in control, they are basically back in school. This is why your blog is of such value for your business, people feel comfortable being educated through blogs as it is informal and they are not being lectured.

With informative blog articles, you educate your customers about the industry your niche represent and give them general information about your business and products. Blogging instead of directly confronting your customers with a sales pitch make them feel that you are upfront and honest and that you are interested in their needs and wants.

People prefer reading blog posts than going to your FAQ page on your website. Use your blog to answer questions. A great idea is to create short series of articles that address the most common questions customers have about products, service delivery, and more.

Through your blog posts and comments, you show your store and website visitors that you are approachable and eager to keep communication open between your business and your customers. When your visitors leave comments, do research about their comments and leave encouraging feedback. You get a look into the behavior patterns of your customers and this enables you plan your marketing strategies with a better focus.

Chapter 13: Optimize Your Website for Selling

Search engine optimization is a dreaded concept for many people. They immediately think about complications and technology and the money they will have to spend to get the help of an expert. Yes, SEO can be complicated, but once you understand the basics, the picture becomes a lot clearer and everything you have to do makes sense.

The website for your dropshipping business must be optimized for you to be visible to the search engines. You need a good search ranking to show up high enough when potential customers search for your items or you won't be able to make sales.

Setting your website up for selling and conversions fall under marketing, so it is understandable that many entrepreneurs find it confusing when we speak of optimizing your website for selling. The two concepts work together to bring potential customers to your website and keeping them there long enough to make a sale.

The question most asked is whether SEO can really help to push conversion rates higher. The answer is a definite yes. Once you understand the reasons why your website must be optimized, we will go through each step of the process.

Turn Your Website into a Workhorse

Conversion statistics are not favorable across e-commerce websites and currently stand at 2.5%. This means having a great website that looks good is simply not enough. To get your site traffic to yield a higher conversion rate, you need to study your niche audience and cater to their needs and wants. The way to build customer loyalty is to make your website work as hard as possible. Give your visitors the best possible customer experience with easy site navigation.

This is why you must optimize your website because if your audience cannot find you, there is no possibility of any conversions.

Cater to the Expectations of Your Audience

To give your customers what they want you use lead magnets, give them a reason to want your products. When a visitor comes to your website, let's say your niche is outdoor kitchens, they came to your website because they need a new wood burning stove. When the visitor arrives on your website, he is presented with an in-depth blog article of the advantages of wood burning stoves and the best models for different circumstances. This immediately draws his attention. At the end of the article, you get him to sign up for your email list by offering him a downloadable ebook with decor ideas and information on which models suit different types of outdoor kitchens the best.

A few days later you follow up the lead magnet with for instance a free consultation from a decor expert in his area. You have fulfilled the customer's needs and surpassed his expectations and you have a conversion. This scenario works for whatever your niche products are and whatever incentives are most suitable for your niche products.

Optimization is the key that brings the customer to your website and then your efforts you have put in to appeal to your site visitors will secure you a new customer.

Website Appeal for Your Specific Niche Audience

Your goal and the goal of the search engines are the same, the methods used are simply different. You need to analyze the behavior patterns of the customers in your specific niche, and Google uses over 200 different ranking factors to analyze literally millions of websites, but your goals are the same. To give your website visitors the best possible experience by presenting them with excellent contents and prioritizing the contents that give the best value.

For SEO, you focus on using semantic keywords, the words and phrases used by the person using the search engine to find what he or she is looking for, also called search intent. When you optimize your website for selling with the goal of increased conversions, you guide your website traffic to buy your products, or sign up for your email listings, or join your social media pages.

When you optimize for your website goals and for SEO at the same time, you create a much better working relationship and interaction between the search engines and your website and the result is customer satisfaction.

Organic Traffic

Businesses spend large sums of money every year on paid advertising to attract visitors, when search traffic clicks on one of your sponsored listings or on a paid for advertisement.

Yet, this type of advertising on average leads to a conversion rate of less than 2%.

While it is true that it takes time, effort, and money to develop your website content and to promote it, the organic traffic you gain through SEO is free. The conversion rate for customers that visit your website through organic search is far higher at over 14%.

Investing your time and effort, as well as money, to grow the organic traffic to your website takes time to achieve, and often people are too impatient, they want instant results. The results of paid for advertising is short lived though, but the results from organic traffic are long lasting and brings a far better conversion rate.

Website Data Analysis

The first step in the website optimization process is to analyze your website data. This enables you to see website visitor behavioral patterns that will guide you as to where to apply and focus your SEO.

Google offers the Google Search Console, an excellent tool that gives you user behavior reports such as tracking key metrics for your bounce rate, number of sessions and unique sessions of visitors and the behaviour reports show you how your site visitors behave while they are on your website, which pages they went to the most and which specific pages lead to the best conversion rates.

Keyword Research

Search engine optimization has changed radically, especially in the last decade. You can no longer grab a few keywords you think is suitable and go with that, write an article or two and you get ranked. Today it is a precise science with numerous factors calculated to achieve that sought after first page ranking in the search results.

Ubersuggest is an excellent free keyword search tool for finding keywords that relate to your niche, your niche products and your business. This tool is great for finding long-tail keywords that fit the user intent of your website visitors and prospective customers. With Ubersuggest you are able to use broad keywords and you are then able to filter the keyword results in different ways to get long-tail keywords to target for instance a specific audience within your niche.

There are several tools similar to Ubersuggest, both free and paid for tools, so try out several until you find one that you feel most comfortable with.

Content That Adds Value

We have detailed the importance of offering content that is rich in value in earlier chapters and the benefits you gain. This holds true for SEO and your search engine ranking.

To define what the optimal length of your content is for optimization, run a search for your primary keyword. Visit the top 10 SERPs results for that specific keyword and check the length of those pages. This gives you a good indication of the length of the posts you should concentrate on.

This i s important as it alerts Google that you are providing a significant amount of information and the time people spend on that particular page and this is a positive for your search ranking.

On-Page SEO

Keep on-page optimization clean and simple. The goal of on-page SEO is to use your website design, images, and words to enable the search engines to understand it.

Identify and Strategically Use a Few Relevant Keywords

Use a tool like Ubersuggest to identify a few of the most relevant keywords that describe the core of your niche, or your products. Use the chosen keywords a few times on each page and ensure that the keywords flow naturally in the content. Cramming keywords and key phrases on each page does not help your search ranking as the search engine algorithms are sophisticated and ignore keyword cramming.

Image Optimization

Instead of using the generic "image.jpg" to name image files and alt tags, find relevant ways to use your keywords for image file names and as alt tags. Taking that extra time to optimize your images correctly benefits your on-page SEO.

Internal Links

Internal links are hyperlinks within the content on a page that points to another page on your website that contain relevant information. Internal links spread link equity, in layman's terms called link juice, across your website by transferring page authority on to another page. So if you have certain pages that do not rank high, you can link such a page to a higher ranking webpage with an internal link. Internal links help carry those pages with lower ranking to rank better. Without internal links, the search engine spiders cannot crawl individual pages – the hyperlinks point them to other pages.

An excellent tool is Link Explorer that takes the confusion out of internal linking with several great features and is definitely worth getting if you are not sure how to go about creating internal links.

Mobile Optimization

The graph below shows how strongly the use of mobile devices have increased as the preferred way of accessing the internet in the past few years. It has, therefore, become a necessity for websites to be optimized for mobile users.

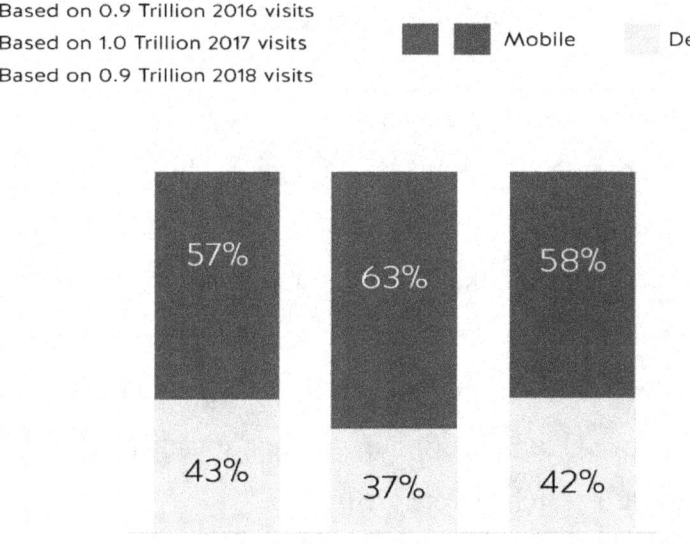

(Perficient Digital, 2019)

Google launched the mobile-first index in 2018, so it is a must to optimize your website to be mobile friendly. Otherwise, you could lose out on a significant percentage of conversions from mobile internet users.

The easiest way to make your website mobile friendly is through responsive design. WordPress takes the worry of coding off your shoulders as they offer free and premium themes that come with responsive design already built-in.

High-Grade Backlinks

Google considers backlinks as a sign of the credibility of your website and this influences your ranking. The rule to remember for backlinks is that it must come from a reputable website. It does not enhance your rating if you have loads of backlinks, but they come from websites that are not trustworthy. Quality definitely trumps quantity when you want to earn search engine credibility.

Getting quality backlinks means work for you as it takes time and effort to cultivate trustworthy backlinks. It is worth it as quality backlinks are SEO gold and with so many ways to get backlinks it can be fun instead of a chore.

One of the most popular ways to get backlinks is through infographics. Create interesting infographics that people want to see and share. Another popular way of getting backlinks is to do guest blogging. Writing great articles on other website blogs earn you backlinks, but also introduces new audiences to your own website and enhances your online reputation.

An interesting way to earn backlinks is to donate to nonprofit organizations. Do a search for any websites within your niche that not only accepts donations, but alo link back to websites from which they received donations.

These are a few ideas of getting quality backlinks, there are many other options to explore. Be creative and do searches for link building opportunities that interest you and fit your niche.

Page Speed

Your site performance, how fast your pages load has a huge impact on SEO and your percentage of customer conversions. Shoppers are not prepared to wait around for a slow webpage to load, and nearly half of all visitors to websites that have slow loading time will lose those potential customers. They abandon the page if it takes three seconds or longer to load.

In 2018, Google added a page speed update to their algorithm, making it critical to ensure your website has fast page loading as this counts for your search page ranking.

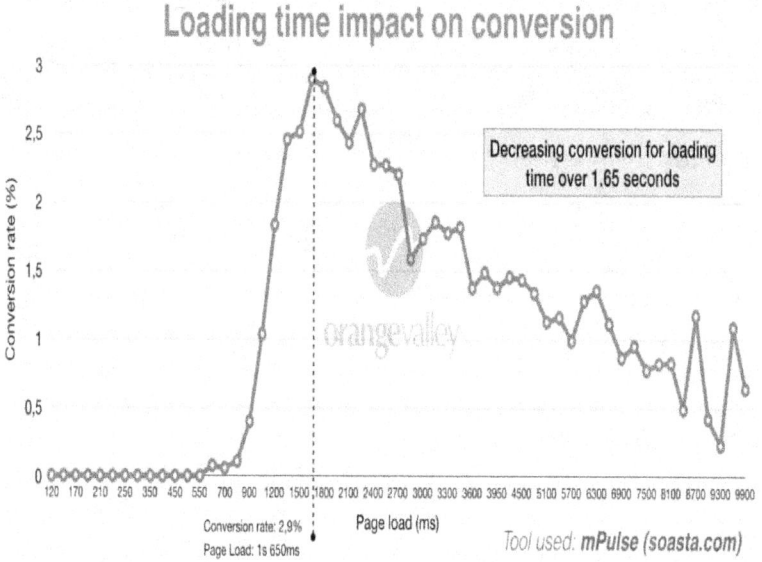

(Soasta Inc, 2010)

To solve the slow page speed and improve your ranking and your conversion rate is not difficult to do.

Page Speed Insights by Google is the best app to use to correct this problem. The app delivers a detailed breakdown of the loading time for your website on mobile devices and desktop computers. Then, the app provides you with step-by-step guidance on how to fix the problems to improve your page loading speed and suggest strategies on how to reduce server calls, to reduce file size and to minimize load speed.

Chapter 14: How to Scale Your Dropshipping Business

Scaling is vital for the success of a dropshipping business. Without growth, your business will stagnate, and that is the beginning of the end of any business. No matter what your personal goals are for your business, whether you want to become a business mogul or settle in and have a comfortable and sustainable business, you have to scale. The whole concept of scaling can be unnerving as you will be moving out of your comfort zone and taking on more responsibilities. However, if you go about scaling your business step-by-step and use all the tools and strategies available, it becomes easy to do and exciting to see your business grow.

Scaling is not a single option only way of growing your business. It is very flexible and if one particular form of scaling does not work for your niche, you have a variety of other options to try out and implement those that fit your particular dropshipping business the best. That is what makes scaling so successful, you can add all the different options that fit, there are no limits.

Are You Ready?

Premature scaling is the phrase used in commerce for expanding your business without first putting into place a solid foundation to build your scaling for your business. It is not only startup businesses that fall into this trap, even long established companies and this invariably leads to failure.

Before you can be ready to scale, you must work through several steps for your scaling efforts to be successful as follows.

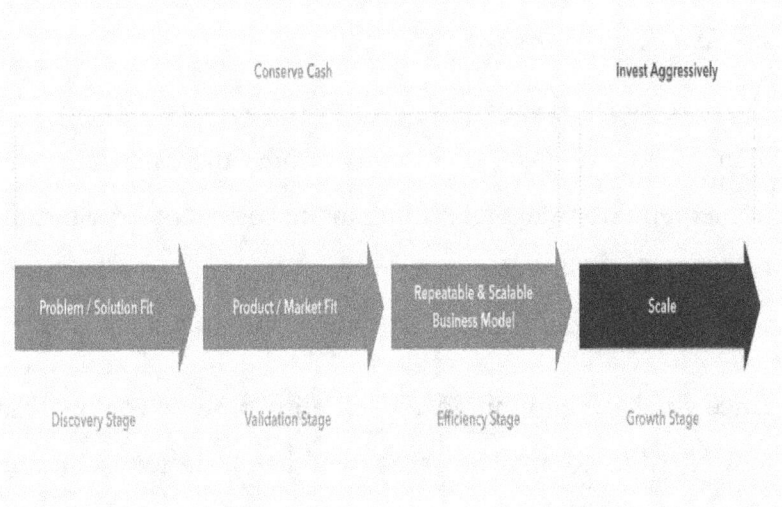

(Hackermoon, 2017)

Cash Safety Net

Build up a cash safety net for your business before you scale to allow for any setbacks during scaling. This will allow you to change strategies during scaling and have the cash to back you up if one strategy does not work out. Without a cash safety net, you won't have the means to try more than one strategy to get the perfect product and market fit.

Logical Steps Forward

You need to take the steps from the start to the implementation stage of scaling in the correct order. Starting at the wrong end of your scaling will result in a lot more work, money spent needlessly and opportunities lost.

Once you have committed to the scaling process you become less flexible to maneuver as you have started spending money on products, hiring a person or people to help run the business and advertising.

To avoid all the problems of premature scaling is not difficult. Do not spend money on non-essentials, save all extra cash to enable you to progress without getting into a cash bind in the middle of scaling. Once you have that set up you make very sure that you know exactly what your customers want and have all the ways to reach potential customers and have set up strategies and advertising to reach all of your potential customers in the target group of your scaling effort. The last step is to test whatever products you want to scale, or new products you want to add to your business. You must base your scaling on proven test results, not guesses or what people say are the latest trends or fads. Once you have all the above in place, you have eliminated the possibility of premature scaling and are indeed ready to start scaling your dropshipping business.

Scaling Vertically

Traditional vertical scaling means you add more products in your niche or expand on the categories in your niche. You also increase your budget for advertising for existing ad sets that are doing extremely well. In short you offer more products, increase your ad spend, but do not focus on finding new audiences to target within your niche. This is a good, solid way of scaling with a proven track record.

Scaling Horizontally

Scaling horizontally give you several options, or combinations of the horizontal scaling options to implement, whichever fits your business best and you find the most comfortable to use. Basically, instead of scaling upwards with your existing products, you scale by introducing your products to new audiences – you scale wide.

Become Your Own Franchise

You duplicate your existing business and online store to open up the opportunity to sell to clients in your niche who speak another language. If you speak more than one language, you can manage this yourself by simply translating everything on your existing website to the target language.

If you do not speak another language, go into partnership with someone who speaks your target language and share profits for the new franchise website on a 50% basis with this person.

Duplicating your business in another language has greater appeal to people where the official language is not English. Shoppers in Europe, the Balkan countries and the Far East prefer to shop online in their own language and prefer the Euro as payment currency.

The benefit of duplicating is that you will have a higher conversion rate, but you also take on a lot more work and you will be limited in how many countries you can target in your scaling efforts.

Keep It English and Go Global

Scaling globally and keeping everything in English has the drawback of losing potential clients who do not want to do business in English and use USD as the currency for payment, giving you a lower conversion rate.

To offset this drawback, scale globally for the countries where English is the official language or one of the official languages. This form of global scaling is a lot less work than duplicating your website, freeing up time to concentrate on other areas of your business.

Scaling Into Neighboring Niches

This is a great way to scale your business, by investigating the niches that borders on your own niche and look for any products in these neighboring niches that would compliment the products that you are already selling. Look for products that the customers in your own niche would be interested in buying and test the reaction to the new products by offering a few at a time. Your sales statistics will clearly show you which products your niche customers like best and then you can make adjustments to the products you offer from neighboring niches.

You can do this form of scaling indefinitely without spending extra on advertising before you are sure that any neighboring niche products are viable to be added permanently.

Facebook Lookalike Audiences

Facebook offers a segmentation tool that creates lookalike audiences based on the followers that you currently have.

The tool takes the interest and demographics of your followers to create a lookalike audience that you can target. As the demographics and interests of the new audience closely match that of your current followers, this form of scaling enables focussed marketing and finds you groups with a very high potential conversion rate.

Facebook uses its massive user base to look for similarities to create a lookalike audience that would never be found without the user data stored within Facebook. This tool works as long as you have a minimum of 100 people in your client group, but the larger your total is, the more effective this tool becomes.

You can create your lookalike audience from your customer lists, your website traffic and the fan pages you have and select different types of lookalike audiences.

Specific Demographics

You can refine your demographics for the lookalike audience by setting certain parameters such as specific location, gender, and age group for an even narrower focus to target your advertising.

Audience Size Selection

Select the large audience option to maximize the number of people you reach that similar to your current audience gives you a much broader audience, but there will be less similarities shared than your fans and current customers have in common.

When you select a smaller lookalike audience, it will result in a smaller number of people seeing your ads, but those people will share far more characteristics with your fans and clients.

Facebook CBO

In September 2019, Facebook introduced a new feature for optimizing how your advertising budget is distributed, the campaign budget optimization (CBO) feature. This algorithm now does real time optimization of your ad budget across your ad sets. It targets the best opportunities separately, optimizing them one-by-one on what it deems to be the least expensive cost per result. Once done with an opportunity, it moves on to the next best opportunity. It does not take into consideration the amount spent on the previous ad set. The benefit of CBO is that the algorithm targets your top performing ad sets and you no longer waste money on opportunities that are much less likely to lead to sales and conversions by intelligently optimizing your campaign budget to target the ads that perform the best and the audiences that respond the best.

Google Similar Audiences and Customer Match

Google offers several tools that assist you in re-engaging customers and scaling your business.

Customer Match uses your data, both offline and online, that customers have shared with you to enable you to re-engage customers across Display, YouTube, Search, Gmail, and Shopping. This tool can also target other potential clients similar to those you already have.

The Similar Audiences tool from Google, works on the same lines as the Facebook Lookalike tool. The searches for Similar Audiences most often uses your marketings lists, first-party data information to target new users who have share similar characteristics, and interests of your best performing website visitors groups.

Estimate and Plan

Planning ahead is crucial for scaling to be successful. To enable you to plan with accuracy, you must do two specific forecast evaluations. It is important to be as thorough as possible with as much data as possible to give you the best realistic results.

A customer growth forecast, broken down into categories with specifics such as number of new clients, estimated number of orders and broken down by different months.

An expense forecast on similar lines as the sales growth forecast as to what systems you have in place and will need to cope with the extra number of orders. Also what changes will be needed to your infrastructure, what upgrades in technology you will need, and the extra manpower needed to cope with running the business during your scaling period.

Suppliers

A vital part of scaling your business is your suppliers. You must be able to trust that your suppliers are able to scale with you and that you will not find yourself in the middle of your scaling operation having to deal with a supplier who cannot keep up with your increased orders. Make absolutely sure your supplier can keep up, especially if your scaling involves custom products or new products on the market. Should you have doubts about the supplier's ability, it is wise to search for a new supplier or a backup supplier.

When you start scaling communicate with your suppliers, you bring them into the picture. Suppliers are totally aware of the benefits your scaling will bring to their own business. They would prefer that you stay loyal to them, so negotiate the best prices for the products you are scaling. If you have built a solid business relationship with your suppliers, the majority of them will be open to negotiations.

Support Staff

As your business grows and orders increase, you need support staff as you will reach a stage where you can no longer handle the orders coming, customer queries and placing orders on your own. No business can afford to have a bad relationship with clients and especially new clients. You need to have a competent person or persons in place who will be able to help you deal with customer queries and communicate with and place orders with your suppliers.

A cost-effective way to have the needed support staff in place is to outsource by hiring a virtual assistant or virtual assistants for your specific business requirements. You can train and introduce your virtual assistant to your suppliers and you do not have to spend money on extras such as office space and equipment. This means you can use the money in your cash safety net for other needs within your business.

Technology and Automation

Automation is top of the list for the smooth running of any dropshipping company, and doubly so during the process of scaling. There simply is no time to do tasks manually as it is too time consuming, leaving you with little or no time to concentrate on the many extra tasks that need to be done to scale successfully.

Two forms of automation to put in place before you start scaling is to automate order fulfilment and auto order tracking. These to automation options keep orders being placed going and keep customers happy as they can track the progress of their orders. Tracking is especially beneficial when you are dealing with first time customers who may be uncomfortable dealing with a company they do not really know.

Make sure that you integrate as many of your systems as possible to prevent communications problems. The more unintegrated systems you have, the higher the chances are that the systems will not function well together, so prevent problems further along the line by integrating your systems to the greatest extent possible

Chapter 15: Pitfalls and Mistakes to Avoid

We have purposefully left this section for last. This is not a doom and gloom chapter; this is your go to section and refer back to often when issues crop up. Everything we discuss here is to help you navigate the inevitable pitfalls you will come across when you start your own dropshipping business and how to avoid falling into the traps so many dropshippers before you have.

Dropshipping businesses do not fail because people are stupid. Everyone wants to succeed and this puts a lot of pressure on you when you start out. People make mistakes because they become impatient to succeed and take shortcuts with disastrous consequences. The biggest mistakes in the success of a dropshipping business often happens because you simply do not know what to look out for and what to avoid.

The important thing to keep in mind with this chapter is that people before you have made these mistakes and some have given up on or suffered financial loss. They have been there, they have done that and you can learn from them. This chapter is to help you safely navigate the intricate maze of e-commerce successfully.

Not Learning from Mistakes

You are human and will make mistakes. The number one mistake that entrepreneurs can make is to learn nothing from the mistakes made. Nobody starts out having all the information about dropshipping; you learn as you go along and if you make mistakes, you learn from them. When an issue crops up, you find solutions and ways to avoid making that same mistake again. When you choose not to learn or make no effort to find out how to correct problems and mistakes, you set your dropshipping business up for failure.

Customers, Audience

When you start your dropshipping business, you need to know what your market. Thinking that having products in the latest trend is going to automatically be successful does not work. You need to know exactly who your target audience is, guessing is a costly mistake. Research is key; you must gather statistical data about your niche audience and get to know everything possible about them.

In Chapter 12, we discussed cross-selling and upselling as market strategies. Not upselling is a mistake many dropshipping companies still making. Get to know your target audience well enough to generate sales from upselling or your profit margin will stay limited. Have a solid upselling plan ready and don't only rely on your front-end products to generate sales. Upselling is far more cost-effective marketing as you do not spend money advertising these products.

To bring in real money for your business, you need value your previous customers. You have already made the connection and a sale, neglecting to keep in contact through your email lists is a huge mistake to make. Do not focus only on getting new customers, staying in touch with your previous customers form a large part of your overall profit margin.

One of the biggest mistakes newbies make is to try to take on the whole world when they start their dropshipping business. You need to learn to walk before you can run, so focus on your target audience within the USA. Get to know your target audience in the USA where you have a vast niche audience with fast and trustworthy shipping. Once you have established your USA market and gained experience, you can think of going global.

Website

Two mistakes that pop up regularly regarding the dropshipping business store and website are the website structure and product descriptions and names that are badly edited.

Stores and websites that are not neatly and logically set up confuse prospective customers and they soon leave. Not everyone is proficient in coding and HTML or the solution is available. Shopify has all the apps and plugins available to set a store up that functions well and Woocommerce plugin on WordPress system is available for more experienced entrepreneurs.

Dropshipping business that use online platforms such as Alibaba and Aliexpress and use plugins to import product to their store and website do not realize that product names and descriptions must be edited. The descriptions and product names are not relevant to your own dropshipping business, it must be edited to focus your target audience.

SEO

Despite all the information available about search engine optimization and knowing the critical role this plays in online visibility and the conversion rate of a business, this is still a huge problem. Neglecting any aspects of SEO has a long-term negative influence on your business. If you feel you are not able to do it alone, use the many apps and plugins available.

Niche

The two niche mistakes most often made are selecting a niche without in-depth research into that niche and to select too broad a niche. Doing no research means often selecting the wrong niche after setting up and branding your store. This mistake is very costly as you then have to start over from scratch. Selecting too broad a niche is disastrous for marketing, promotions, and SEO when you cannot used precise and focussed keywords.

Brand Visibility

Brand visibility is just as important for your dropshipping business as for any other retail company. It is a mistake to not keep your brand as visible as possible at every opportunity. Custom external packaging, a thank you note after delivery, and sending out customer satisfaction surveys are simple, yet effective, ways to keep your brand visible.

Customer Support

Bad customer support ruins your business. Your customers and potential customers must be priority one and failing to deal fast and efficient with customer complaints, queries and questions labels your business as a company to avoid, especially on social media.

Unrealistic Expectations

Going into dropshipping idealistically thinking it's easy money with little or no effort has been the downfall of many startup businesses. Go into the business with your eyes wide open. Make sure you know how to market your products, who your target audience is, how to compete with the many competitors out there, and be prepared to put in effort is the recipe for success.

A mistake often made is thinking that once you have set up your online store and created a website, that is all you have to do, and from there on, you will earn a passive income. If you do nothing, that is exactly what happens, nothing.

Giving up if you don't show immediate success or when a strategy fails. No business has instant success or are without failures, it takes perseverance and time to succeed.

Not being able to accept negative feedback from clients on social media platforms, your store, and website. Negative feedback is not a personal attack, all businesses get negative feedback; it does not mean your business is a failure. Work with the negative feedback, find solutions and move on.

Trademarked Goods

Selling trademarked products has been the downfall of many dropshipping business. The trademark laws in the USA and the EU are very strict and harsley enforced, it is simply not worth it to lose everything you worked for plus the chance of being sued.

Suppliers

Overdependence on a single supplier happens when an entrepreneur is comfortable with a supplier who has given good service over time. Anything can happen, from stock shortages, sudden massive price increases or the supplier has had an influx of orders and are unable to fulfill them all. It is wise to always have a backup supplier, even if your niche is tightly focussed.

Marketing

The top reason dropshipping companies use poor marketing strategies happens because they do not know their niche customers well enough. This results in their marketing being promoted to everyone instead of focussing tightly on their niche customers.

Another mistake is promoting their products randomly without researching the specific channels where most of their customers are active. Random marketing results are mediocre at best with very low returns.

Legal Liabilities and Taxes

Legal liabilities is a pitfall especially for startup companies and many try to ignore this. The solution to avoid legal liabilities is to register your dropshipping business as a company. Once you are legally registered as a business, the company and not you personally are liable for all agreements, contracts, and all business deals.

Sales tax is confusing and leads to numerous mistakes. Shopify and Woocommerce platforms assist sellers who open shops on their platforms with settings that automatically collects the sales taxes due on products.

Handling Orders

When you start your business it is easy to fall into the trap of manually fulfilling orders and many people do. This works well in the beginning, but as soon as the business starts growing, they can no longer keep up. Save yourself a lot of frustration with an app such as Oberlo that automates your order fulfilling.

People make mistakes when they shop online, they change their minds about which product they want or they want to cancel an order. It is your duty to make sure this process is handled correctly and professionally to ensure customer satisfaction. Ensure that your supplier confirms with you about any changes and then confirm with the customer that changes have been made, or the correct refunds will be applied.

Conclusion

Everything you need to start your dropshipping business is now in your hands. Start small and dream big. You know what to look out for and steer clear of. Many people have a macabre need to give entrepreneur unsolicited advice by telling horror stories of failure and wasting money by starting a dropshipping business venture. Do not listen to them.

Building your dropshipping business takes time, it does not happen in the blink of an eye. Success will follow when your biggest investment is yourself. Your efforts, your time, your determination and your drive to succeed.

It is normal to feel overwhelmed when you start. Remember though, each step you take is a step forward. The most difficult part of owning a dropshipping company is to actually start. It does not matter if you are uncertain about things; most people are plain scared to start up a company.

Start out right and half the battle is won. Think smart and don't rush into things and then having to backtrack and fix the mistakes you have made. Use every tool available to you to take advantage of all the features of the dropshipping software that fits your niche.

The dropshipping business model is incredibly popular despite all the doom and gloom people insisting it is not a sustainable business model. Remember, Jeff Bezos started in a tiny office, with computer wires everywhere and a handwritten banner on the wall with his company name, and Bill Gates started in his garage.

www.ingramcontent.com/pod-product-compliance
Lightning Source LLC
Chambersburg PA
CBHW070629220526
45466CB00001B/135